CAMBRIDGE OFFICIAL PREPARATION MATERIAL

Cambridge English

Fun for Flyers

Student's Book
Fourth edition

Anne Robinson
Karen Saxby

Cambridge University Press
www.cambridge.org/elt

Cambridge Assessment English
www.cambridgeenglish.org

Information on this title: www.cambridge.org/9781316632000

© Cambridge University Press & Assessment 2016

First published 2006
Second edition 2010
Third edition 2015
Fourth edition 2016

40 39 38 37 36 35 34 33 32 31 30 29

Printed in Dubai by Oriental Press

A catalogue record for this publication is available from the British Library

ISBN 978-1-316-61758-8 Student's Book with online activities with audio and Home Fun booklet
ISBN 978-1-316-63200-0 Student's Book with online activities with audio
ISBN 978-1-316-61760-1 Teacher's Book with downloadable audio
ISBN 978-1-108-72814-0 Presentation Plus

The authors and publishers would like to thank the ELT professionals who commented on the material at different stages of its development.

The authors are grateful to: Niki Donnelly of Cambridge University Press.

Anne Robinson would like to give special thanks to Adam Evans and her parents Margaret and Jim and to many, many teachers and students who have inspired her along the way. Special thanks to Cristina and Victoria for their help, patience and enthusiasm. And in memory of her brother Dave.

Karen Saxby would like to give special thanks to everyone she has worked with at Cambridge Assessment since the birth of YLE! She would particularly like to mention Frances, Felicity and Ann Kelly. She would also like to acknowledge the enthusiasm of all the teachers she has met through her work in this field. And lastly, Karen would like to say a big thank you to her sons, Tom and William, for bringing constant FUN and creative thinking to her life and work.

Freelance editorial services by Katrina Gormley

Design and typeset by Wild Apple Design.

Cover design by Chris Saunders (Astound).

Sound recordings by dsound Recording Studios, London

The authors and publishers acknowledge the following sources of copyright material and are grateful for the permissions granted. While every effort has been made, it has not always been possible to identify the sources of all the material used, or to trace all copyright holders. If any omissions are brought to our notice, we will be happy to include the appropriate acknowledgements on reprinting and in the next update to the digital edition, as applicable.

The authors and publishers are grateful to the following illustrators:

T = Top, B = Below, L = Left, R = Right, C = Centre, B/G = Background

The authors and publishers are grateful to the following illustrators:

Akbar Ali (The Organisation) pp. 6 (B), 7 (R), 10, 11, 23 (B), 24 (B), 25, 35 (B), 39 (B), 44 (B), 52, 81, 85 (T), 104 (R), 105 (B), 114, 115; Laetitia Aynié (Sylvie Poggio Artists Agency) pp. 12, 40 (BL), 73, 97, 101 (BR); David Banks pp. 65, 79, 99; Bridget Dowty (Graham-Cameron Illustration) pp. 33 (T), 39 (T), 67, 96; Andy Elkerton (Sylvie Poggio Artists Agency) pp. 14, 19, 34 (TL), 85 (B); Chris Embleton-Hall (Advocate Art) pp. 20, 22, 54 (B), 75 (CR); Pablo Gallego (Beehive Illustration) pp. 13 (B), 21 (B), 27 (T), 32, 57, 66 (B), 91, 100 (BR), 101 (C), 102 (B), 126, 128 (BR); Daniela Geremia (Beehive Illustration) pp. 8 (C), 18 (B), 36 (B), 69 (B), 106 (T); John Haslam pp. 7 (BC), 8 (T), 13 (T), 14 (TL), 16, 17 (B), 46, 50 (B), 58, 59 (C), 61 (C), 68 (B), 82 (B), 90 (C), 110, 111 (T); Brett Hudson (Graham-Cameron Illustration) pp. 48 (B), 49 (TR), 106 (R), 107 (B); Nigel Kitching (Sylvie Poggio Artists Agency) pp. 26 (T), 29 (T), 94, 105 (R); Gustavo Mazali (Beehive Illustration) pp. 9, 14 (B), 17 (T), 21 (T), 44 (T), 45, 50 (T), 51, 54 (T), 59 (T), 79, 82 (T), 98, 104 (TR), 112 (CR), 122, 124, 126, 128 (T); Bethan Matthews (Sylvie Poggio Artists Agency) p 93Nina de Polonia (Advocate Art) pp. 15,24 (TR), 35 (T), 40 (T), 48 (T), 56 (C), 61 (TR), 69 (T), 74, 90 (BL); Pulsar Studios (Beehive Illustration) pp. 53, 64 (BR), 95 (T), 109, 119, 121; Anthony Rule pp. 5, 6 (T), 7 (BR), 17 (BL), 24 (R), 29 (B), 31 (B), 33 (B), 42, 47 (B), 49 (B), 51, 52, 56 (T), 59 (B), 61 (BR), 70 (T), 75 (BR), 76, 77 (BR), 85 (BR), 90 (T), 92 (T), 95 (R), 100 (T), 106 (TR), 111 (BR), 112 (T), 116 (T), 123 (BR) 125 (BR); Pip Sampson pp. 11, 23 (T), 28, 37, 55, 62, 63, 66, 67, 68 (T), 86, 87,107 (T), 127 (C); Alberto Saichann (Beehive illustrations) p53; Will Saxby p. 73 (TR); Melanie Sharp (Sylvie Poggio Artists Agency) pp. 18 (T), 26 (B), 27 (B), 30, 31 (T), 34 (TC), 47 (T), 70 (B), 71, 72, 75 (T), 84, 92 (BR), 93, 102, 103, 113, 116 (B), 117; Emily Skinner (Graham-Cameron Illustration) pp. 88 (T), 89 (C), 108; Lisa Smith p. 36; Jo Taylor p. 42; Theresa Tibbetts (Beehive Illustration) p. 92 (TL); Matt Ward (Beehive illustration) pp 66 (T), 68 (B a,e,g); Tatio Viana (Advocate Art) pp. 38, 41, 47 (C), 64 (T), 76, 77 (T), 88 (B), 89 (T), 99, 106 (B), 123 (T), 125.

Contents

1 Hello again

A Look at the picture. Where are these? Draw lines.

the sky   the seat   the skateboard   the backpack   the roof

the bicycle   the grass   the sunglasses

B Say how the pictures are different.

C Look at the picture in B. Write the missing words.

The seven people in the picture are about ¹...................... years old. The girl in the orange sweater is standing on a ²...................... . Robert is sitting on the ³...................... . He is interested in ⁴...................... . A girl and a boy are standing beside ⁵...................... . It's blue.

D ▶ Listen and write the answers.

	Robert's favourite game	
Example	Name of game:	...........Silver Moon...........
1	When got this game:	last ....
2	Played this game with:	his ....
3	Name of alien in game:	....
4	Colour of alien's feet:	....
5	Alien likes finding:	....

E Find the answer to each question. Draw lines.

1 How do you get to school in the morning?

2 Do you play video games in your classroom sometimes?

3 What do you and your friends like chatting about?

4 Where do you like going with your friends?

5 Which clothes do you like wearing most?

6 What's your favourite colour?

a I think it's blue, but I like black, too.
b I like jeans and T-shirts best.
c Our favourite place is the playground.
d We can't do that in the lessons.
e Our newest apps and the people in our class at school.
f I ride my bicycle, but not every day.
g No, my friend likes yellow most.

PROJECT

F Let's say!

round clouds and brown cows!

2 Wearing and carrying

A Write letters to make words under the pictures. Where do we wear these? Draw lines.

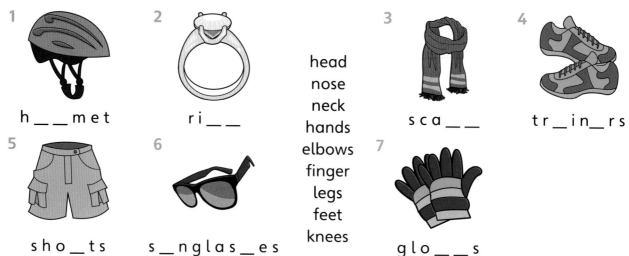

1 h _ _ m e t

2 r i _ _

head
nose
neck
hands
elbows
finger
legs
feet
knees

3 s c a _ _ _

4 t r _ i n _ r s

5 s h o _ t s

6 s _ n g l a s _ e s

7 g l o _ _ _ s

B Read the sentences and write the correct words from the box.

| a watch | an umbrella | gloves | a rucksack | pockets | a coat | a belt |
| a helmet | a backpack | a handbag | suitcases | a uniform | trainers |

1 People can carry things on their back in this.   *a rucksack* / ....

2 You wear this over other clothes when you go outside.   ....

3 Women often carry this. They put things like pens and keys in it.   ....

4 Some school children have to wear this when they go to school.   ....

5 It's a good idea to wear this on your head when you're cycling.   ....

6 When you want to know the time, look at this.   ....

7 Lots of people put these on their feet before they do sports.   ....

8 When it rains, you can open this so you don't get wet.   ....

9   People carry things in these when they are travelling. Some
    have little wheels.   ....

10 Some people wear this round the top of their trousers or skirt. ....

11 We put these on our hands in cold weather.   ....

12 If you're wearing trousers, you can keep small things in these. ....

C Look and read. Circle the correct word.

1 The queen is wearing a very pretty ~~necklace~~ / _belt_.
2 _Three_ / _four_ long, thin flags are flying in the wind.
3 One person is carrying a big plate with _fruit_ / _noodles_ on it.
4 The man with the message is wearing boots on his _knees_ / _feet_.
5 You can see a large _round_ / _square_ table in the castle garden.
6 The king has a wonderful gold _crown_ / _hat_ on the top of his head.

D ▶ Who are the people at the castle? Listen and draw lines.

Mary

Peter

Oliver

....

Helen

Sarah

....

Michael

Harry

E ▶ Listen again. Answer the questions.

1 What is the name of the castle?
2 Who listens to the king's secrets?
3 Who is the queen's best friend?
4 Who is the important letter for?

F Funtime Play the game! Why are you together?

3 Spots and stripes

A Talk about the flags in the picture.

B Complete the sentences about the second picture. Use 1, 2 or 3 words.

Example   There's one boat and it's got three green flags with ..grey.sharks.. on them.

1   The man with the beard isn't wearing .... on his feet.
2   The boys are carrying large .... in their right hands.
3   The child who's wearing pink and yellow shorts is .... the boat.
4   The .... is coming out from behind the clouds.
5   .... on the boy's shoulder has blue and yellow stripes on it.

C Look at the pictures in A and B. What differences can you see?

D Look at the picture. Write your own answers to the questions. Write one sentence about the picture at the end.

1   How old are the four children? ....
2   Why is one of the passengers crying? ....
3   What's in the suitcases? ....
4   What's the man reading about? ....
5   What song is the boy in the jacket listening to? ....

6   **Now write one sentence about this airport picture.**
Write about the passengers or the airport building.

....
....

E ▶ **Look at the picture in D. Listen and colour and write.**

F Can you find the picture I've written about?

4 My friends and my pets

A **Let's talk about your friends and family.**

1 Who lives in your house? Who's the oldest person in your house?
2 Has anyone in your family got your name too?
3 Who sits next to you in class? Do you and your classmates always sit in the same seat?
4 Which friends do you see at the weekend? What do you do with your friends at the weekend?
5 Tell me about your best friend at school. What does she/he look like? Tell me about her/his hobbies.

B ▶ **What does Holly say about her friends?**
Listen, write names, then draw lines.

1 .... Jane ....   a   also has guitar lessons.
2 ....   b   is in the same class.
3   c   is Holly's cousin.
4 ....   d   is Holly's best friend.
5 ....   e   likes the same music.
6 ....   f   is very funny.
7 ....   g   goes sailing too.
8 ....   h   is a loud singer.

C **Now write the names of people you know.**

1 .... likes the music I like.
2 .... is the funniest person in this class.
3 .... is a really great singer.
4 .... is very good at sport.

12

D Read the email and write the missing words. Write one word on each line.

Hi Hugo!

Come and see our new house next week! Monday's
...........*the*........... best day.

Example

1   It's quite easy to get here .... bus because it stops
on the corner of our street. You can also meet our new pet!
It's so cool! It's green and red and really sweet but it's much

2   naughtier .... your pet rabbit! It takes grapes and

3   bits .... bread from the kitchen table sometimes!

4   .... the weather's OK, we can watch the football

5   match in King's Park. .... is your
favourite football team?

See you!
Sally

E ▶ Listen and write the names.

Monday – Go to friend's house!
1   Name: .....*Sally*.............
2   Bus stop is in: .... Street
3   Sally's house is in: .... Road
4   Name of house: ....
5   Sally's dog's name: ....
6   Sally's parrot's name: ....

F Where are the 'h's?

5 About animals

A How do they move? Write the animals below each word.

kangaroo   bat   ~~mouse~~   crocodile   goat   dolphin   jellyfish   bee   penguin   zebra

run	fly	jump	swim	hop
mouse	....	....	....	....
....	....	....	....	....
....	....	....	....	....
....	....	....	....	....
....	....	....	....	....

B Look and read. Choose the correct word and write it on the line.

butterflies
a camel
dinosaurs
a bee
an octopus
swans
~~a rabbit~~
a beetle
a donkey
a polar bear
a tortoise

1 This wild animal usually has grey fur and when it feels
   frightened, it hops away very quickly.   ....a rabbit.......

2 This is an insect that works hard to make honey.   ....

3 This animal has a long neck and can carry heavy bags for a
   long time in hot, dry places.   ....

4 These big birds are usually white. They have long necks and
   live near rivers and lakes.   ....

5 This animal lives in the sea and has eight long arms.   ....

6 These have wings with lots of different colours on them.
   They fly and sit on plants and flowers.   ....

7 This large, white, furry animal lives in cold countries.   ....

8 This creature walks very slowly and has a large shell on its back.   ....

C Choose the right words and write them on the lines.

Dinosaurs

Example	Dinosaurs .....*lived*..... on our planet 65,000,000 years ago! The first dinosaurs		living	lives	lived
1	.... like big lizards. Many of them	1	looks	looked	looking
2	had short tails, big heads .... walked on four legs. Most dinosaurs were herbivores, which means that they only ate plants. Some of these dinosaurs were very	2	and	because	than
3	.... but other kinds of dinosaur were bigger and heavier and were carnivores, which means that they ate meat. Dinosaurs	3	small	smaller	smallest
4	lived .... warm forests where there	4	to	in	from
5	were lots and lots .... plants and water. But about 60,000,000 years ago, some	5	off	out	of
6	people say .... weather on Earth suddenly got colder and drier. Many plants	6	the	one	those
7	.... dinosaurs liked to eat stopped growing, which was a terrible problem for these animals, so soon dinosaurs disappeared too.	7	what	that	who
8	Today, people sometimes .... dinosaur teeth in rocks or under the ground. Dinosaurs are now extinct, but you can	8	finds	found	find
9	learn about .... in special science museums or when you watch scary dinosaur	9	they	their	them
10	films .... TV.	10	at	by	on

D Do you know the missing word?

Lots .... dinosaurs   a story .... a dolphin

1 all kinds .... bats
2 a book .... the jungle
3 a pair .... wings

4 this part .... the story
5 a cartoon .... wild animals
6 a song .... a dolphin

E Funtime Play the game! Dolphins or bats?

6 My things

A **What are these? Write words on the lines next to the pictures.**

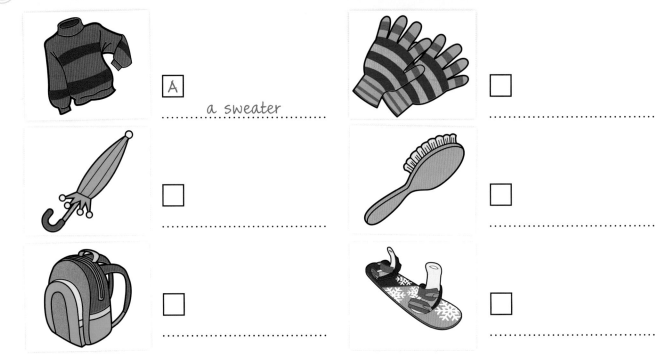

A   .... a sweater ....

☐   ....

☐   ....

☐   ....

☐   ....

☐   ....

B ▶ **Listen. Which animal is on each thing in A? Write a letter (A–H).**

A   B   C   D

E   F   G   H

C ▶ **Match, then colour the two parts of the sentences.**

A	Betty's mother decided to buy this sweater	from a shop in the mountains.
B	Her friend Mary chose this and	on her camping holiday last summer.
C	Her father got her this in January	Betty's fingers and hands don't get cold.
D	Her grandmother made these so	at the zoo shop last year.
E	Her friend, Clare, bought her this because	Betty always brushes her hair with it.
F	Betty carried her things in this	Betty loves these sea creatures.

D **Ask and answer questions about some more of Betty's things.**

A **Betty's keyboard**

Colour?	silver
When/get?	last Saturday
New/old?	new
Who/gave?	aunt
Where/now?	upstairs

B **Betty's violin**

New/old?	old
Where/now?	downstairs
Who/gave?	grandfather
When/get?	last birthday
Colour?	light brown

E *Funtime* **Let's do an animal quiz!**

PROJECT

7 Moving and speaking

A Write eyes, ears, mouth, nose or hands next to the words.

bounce	hands	smell		catch		cry	
shout		see		cook		whistle	
carry		throw		hear		whisper	
speak		call		watch		sing	
push		laugh		pull		hold	
build		clap		chat		taste	

B Complete each sentence with a word from the word box.

> whisper   hear   believe   Describe   guess   decide

1 Could you speak more loudly, please? I can't .... you.
2 .... your school uniform to me. What does it look like?
3 My friends sometimes .... secrets to me in class!
4 I can't .... which pyjamas to wear. My red ones or my grey ones?
5 Dad doesn't always .... me when I say my bedroom's tidy!
6 Can you .... the name of my favourite tune?

C Look at the pictures and tell the story.

1    2    3

4    5

D Read the story. Choose a word from the box.
Write the correct word next to numbers 1–5.

Example
city cloudy whistled actor wings climbed animals sausages excited built

I'm Helen. I live in the
............*city*............ but last August
I visited my new school friend,
David, who lives on a farm
in the north of the country.
His dad, William, is a famous
(1) ...., but he's a
farmer too! I saw lots of cows
and other (2) .... there,
but I remember Pirate, the black
and white sheep dog, most.

Early one morning, David's dad
came into the kitchen. 'The sheep
in the west field aren't there
now!' he said. 'I must find them.
Come and help me!' David and I
jumped up and followed him outside. We all (3) .... up onto
the back of his big old green tractor. Pirate jumped up into the front.

William drove the tractor up the hill. Suddenly, Pirate got very (4) ....
William stopped the engine and shouted, 'Go, Pirate! Find the sheep!' Pirate jumped
down and ran behind some trees. A minute later, we saw him again. The clever dog
ran around the sheep to make them come back down into the west field.

David's dad (5) .... loudly and called, 'Well done, Pirate! Brilliant!'

Pirate worked very hard that day. 'He's tired,' I whispered to David after dinner.
'He ran a long way today.' But Pirate wasn't too tired to eat some of his favourite
cookies that evening!

6 Now choose the best name for this story. Tick (✔) one box.
Pirate loses his biscuits   ☐
Pirate helps on the farm   ☐
Pirate drives a tractor   ☐

E Write words to complete the sentences.

8 School subjects

A Write a, e, i, o or u.

_a_ r t   g _ _ _ g r _ p h y   h _ s t _ r y   s p _ r t

l _ n g _ _ g _ s   m _ t h s   m _ s _ c   s c _ _ _ n c _

B Choose the correct words from A and write them on the lines.

1   Teachers might tell you famous facts about the past in this lesson.   ....

2   You have to count and perhaps add numbers together in
this subject.   ....

3   When you study this, you might learn about rocks or caves.   ....

4   You practise talking and listening to your partner and learn
new words in these lessons.   ....

5   Some students learn to play different instruments and tunes
in this class.   ....

C Complete these sentences about art.

artists
draw
paintings
drawing
paints

1   Your teacher shows you how to .... with pencils in this lesson.

2   If you are very good at .... you usually enjoy doing this!

3   You sometimes use brushes, clean water and .... in this class.

4   In this subject, some students look at .... by famous .... Do you?

D Write sentences about sport and science.

....

.... 21

E ▶ **Listen and write.**

	Monday	
Example	Meet in:	the town ....square........
1	See art by:	Alex ....
2	Bus number:	....
3	Sport to read about:	....
4	Time parents should come:	....
5	For lunch, can have:	....

F Read the email and write the missing words.
Write one word on each line.

Hi Matt,

Example I ....'m....... sending you this email because you weren't at school today.

1 In Mr Park's class, we had .... answer some questions about the pyramids in a quiz. It was very interesting! Some of them are 5000 years

2 .... ! I'd like to do a project about them. Did you know that? For

3 homework, we must .... out more things about them. So, look for

4 pictures .... the pyramids or read more about them on your tablet.

You could write something about them too if

5 you like, but not more .... 100 words.

See you tomorrow!
Frank

G Answer the questions. Then choose the best answers for the conversation.

9 In my classroom

A Find the two halves of the sentences.

1 Glue: When you break a cup or plate,
2 Scissors: They are usually made of metal and
3 A dictionary: When you don't understand a word,
4 A bin: When something is old and you don't want it,
5 A calendar: To help you to remember a special day,
6 A file: You keep information in

a you can use them to cut thin card or plastic.
b look in this to find out what it means.
c you can try to repair it with this.
d draw a circle round the date on this.
e this on a computer or laptop.
f it's a good idea to put it in this.

B ▶ Listen and tick (✔) the box.

Example Where can William sit now?

A ☐   B ✔   C ☐

1 What's the first lesson today?

A ☐   B ☐   C ☐

2 What should the students take to their art class?

A ☐   B ☐   C ☐

3 What did William forget to bring to school?

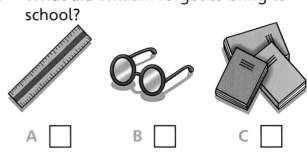

A ☐   B ☐   C ☐

4 Where should the students put their dictionaries?

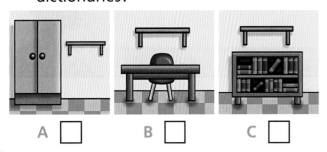

A ☐   B ☐   C ☐

5 What kind of competition is it?

A ☐   B ☐   C ☐

C Look at the pictures and write ee or ea in the words!

1   Miss Sl __e__ __e__ p is showing the qu__ __ n all the gr__ __ n tr__ __ s this w__ __ k.
2   Pl __ __ se make sure your volleyball t__ __m have got c l__ __ n j __ __ ns on!
3   It's r__ __lly __ __ sy for Tom to st__ __ l __ __ch l__ __ f from the tree.
4   In my dr__ __m I had a m__ __ l on the b__ __ ch with a s__ __ monster!
5   Tell the h__ __dteacher that her cakes and brown br__ __d are r__ __dy!
6   We can't carry the h__ __ vy tr __ __sure in this wet w__ __ther.

D Ask and answer questions about different classes.

Michael's class

Name/teacher?	....
How many desks?	....
What/children studying?	....
What/on wall?	....
Lesson easy/difficult?	....

Holly's class

Name/teacher?	....
How many desks?	....
What/children studying?	....
What/on wall?	....
Lesson easy/difficult?	....

E Let's do a pair dictation!

10 Clothes, animals and school

A ▶ **Listen and write.**

	Our school trip!	
Example	Place:	....*butterfly*.... farm
1	Day of trip:	....
2	Went there by:	....
3	Left school at:	.... o'clock
4	Most unusual animal:	a black ....
5	Had a picnic lunch by:	a ....

B Talk about your school trip!

C Look at the picture and write words. Find 16 more things that begin with the same first letter!

PROJECT

a	apple and *animal,*..............	m	mouth and ....
b	book and	n	necklace and ....
c	comic and	p	parrot and ....
d	dress and	r	ring and ....
f	finger and	s	scissors and ....
g	gloves and	t	teacher and ....
h	hair and	u	uniform and ....
i	information and	w	water and ....
l	lizard and		

(D) Look and read. Choose the correct words and write them on the lines.

languages   sunglasses   a bracelet   a dictionary

	You can use this to see the spellings and meanings of words.	...a dictionary...
1	In your music lessons, you might listen to people playing these.	....
2	Women and girls wear these when they go swimming.	....
3	Birds and butterflies use these to help them fly high in the air.	....
4	These are the words and ways people speak in different parts of the world.	....
5	This is perhaps the best animal to ride if you want to cross a desert!	....
6	In this subject you might learn how metals change when they get hot.	....
7	This is the soft coat that animals like rabbits and kittens have on their bodies.	....
8	If you are wearing jeans, you can put your key or phone in this.	....
9	Older students go to this place to learn subjects like history or geography.	....
10	A king might wear this on his head when he is with other important people.	....

fur

wings

swimsuits

a snail

science

a pocket

a crown

instruments   a camel   a college   an insect

(E) Funtime Play the game. What's my word?

11 Visiting different places

A Read the sentences then complete words 2–10 in the S puzzle.

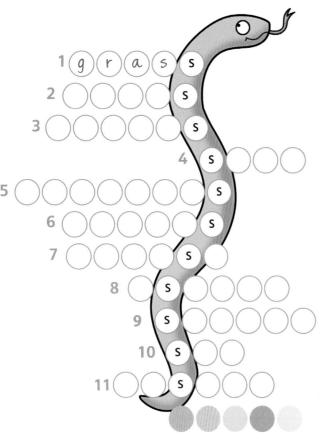

1 (g)(r)(a)(s)(s)
2 ( )( )( )(s)
3 ( )( )( )(s)
4 (s)( )( )( )
5 ( )( )( )( )( )
6 ( )( )( )( )(s)
7 ( )( )( )(s)( )
8 (s)( )( )( )( )
9 (s)( )( )( )( )
10 (s)( )( )( )( )
11 ( )( )(s)( )( )( )

1 This is green and you can usually find it in gardens. Cows eat it!
2 You can walk up these because they're lower than mountains.
3 You find these on farms and some farmers grow vegetables in them.
4 This is usually yellow. It's under your feet when you walk on the beach.
5 People live and work in these places. They're like towns but smaller.
6 You see these on all kinds of plants. They sometimes fall off trees.
7 You can find thousands of tall trees in this place.
8 There is water all round this place so you need a boat to get to it.
9 Most of these are really pretty and you find them on the beach or at the bottom of the sea.
10 When it rains, this is grey and has lots of clouds in it.

B ▶ Listen and colour and write.

C What is Alice saying to her friend, Dan? Choose the best answer.

Dan: Hello, Alice! How are you? Is everything OK?

Alice: _____B_____

1 Dan: Are you camping next to a lake again?

Alice: ....

2 Dan: Who else is there with you?

Alice: ....

3 Dan: Are there any wild animals?

Alice: ....

4 Dan: Where do you sleep at night?

Alice: ....

5 Dan: What about the weather?

Alice: ....

A   I'd like to take the dog for a walk.
B   We're having a wonderful time, thanks! Example
C   My parents, but there are several other people here, too.
D   It changes from cold at night to very hot in the day.
E   We've got tents that have special camping beds inside them.
F   But the water's warm because it was so sunny.
G   That's right. This one's in Yellow Hill Desert, actually.
H   I've seen a crocodile in a river near here.

Dan: ....? Alice: ....

D What's in each rucksack?

gloves   sweater
map   hat   T-shirt
camera   dictionary
chocolate   chess game
torch   sunglasses
phone   umbrella
cold water   blanket

E *Funtime* Play the game! Moving dictation.

12 A journey into space

A Complete the sentences about the picture with words from the box.

1 An astronaut is jumping off the top of the ...._steps_......... .
2 Two of the astronauts are playing .... near the strange tree.
3 The rocket has got small, ... windows.
4 The .... is fixing the computer screen inside the rocket.
5 One of the planets is .... than the other two.
6 The trees have got leaves that look like .... hands.
7 The .... under the rocket looks a bit like sand.

~~steps~~ dark open chess larger robot deeper golf round ground air

B ▶ Listen and write names.

....

C Look at the pictures in A and B. What differences can you see?

D Read the text. Choose the right words and write them on the lines.

Our planet

Example The planet we live ....*on*.... is called
'Earth'. Earth is one of the eight
1 planets .... move around
round and round the sun.

2 Until .... twentieth century, we didn't have
3 .... really good maps of our planet. But now,
4 special cameras in space can .... pictures of
Earth so making maps is easy!

5 .... of our planet has water on it so, in
6 pictures, Earth often .... like a big blue and
white ball!

But pictures of Earth don't only help us to make
7 maps. When we look at ...., we can also
8 learn a .... about the Earth's environment
and weather.

Travelling in space and exploring other planets
9 teaches .... more about Earth, too.

10 .... you like to design spaceships or to be an
astronaut one day?

	on	at	in
1	what	who	that
2	all	the	one
3	lots	any	no
4	take	taking	took
5	Most	Every	Many
6	looks	looking	look
7	they	their	them
8	too	lot	some
9	ours	us	our
10	Can	May	Would

E ▶ Listen and write names, then colour the planets.

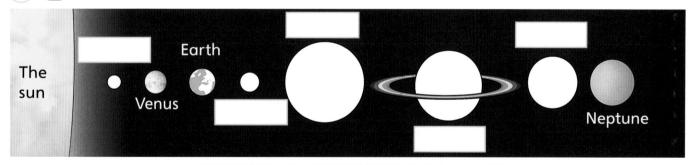

The sun

Earth

Venus

Neptune

Mars   Mercury   Uranus   Saturn   Jupiter

F Answer questions about our planet.

Earth			
What/colour?	blue and white	How long/take/ go round/sun?	365 days, 6 hours and 16 minutes
What/temperature?	about 14°C		
Has/rings?	no	How many/moons?	1

G Let's find out about other planets!

PROJECT

13 What horrible weather!

A Find the weather words.

warmcloudswetwindydryrainhotsunnystormfoggysnowcoldicerainbowtemperature

B ▶ **Listen. Use words from A to complete the sentences.**

1　Alex and his friend can't play volleyball if it starts to .... *rain* ....
2　Dad and Daisy are talking about the noisy .... last night.
3　Mr and Mrs Lime can see a beautiful .... in the sky.
4　Dad wants Helen to remember there might be .... on the ground.
5　Mum says it's dangerous to drive quickly in .... weather.
6　John wants to go out and play in the ....

If it snows, I'd like to ....

C ▶ **Look at the picture. Listen and draw lines.**

Holly　　　　　　Harry　　　　　　Sarah

George　　　　　Emma　　　　　Mark　　　　　Zoe

D Look at the pictures in C and D. What differences can you see?

E ▶ Listen to the first half of the story. What did you hear?

1	Which person says they're getting wet?	Sue	Robert	Michael	Vicky
2	Who is frightened about something?	Sue	Robert	Michael	Vicky
3	Which person is getting cold?	Sue	Robert	Michael	Vicky
4	Whose house can the friends go to?	Sue's	Robert's	Michael's	Vicky's

F ▶ Which picture comes next?

G Look at the last picture and tell the end of the story.

14 Are you hungry? Thirsty?

A **What am I? Find the answers in the word wheels.**

1 A clever insect called a bee makes me!
2 Add me to water to make a really cold drink!
3 I'm made of sugar and fruit. Put me on your bread!
4 I'm made with milk and sometimes fruit like strawberries.
5 I'm white and I look like sand but don't put me in your tea or coffee!

B **Read and guess what Julia is talking about – pasta, sandwiches or fries?**

....

1 You can make this at home with eggs and flour, but I bought a bag of this from a shop. Put it carefully into very hot water and cook it for between five and nine minutes.

2 To make cold ones, put food like salad, eggs or jam between two pieces of bread. Some people like making hot ones with cheese or meat inside.

Complete the sentences about the other food.

3 To make these, you need ...., which you
.... into thin pieces and ....
People eat them with food like ....
.... and ....

32

C ▶ **Listen and tick (✔) the box.**

1   What can Julia have for dinner?   2   What did David have for lunch?

A ☐   B ☐   C ☐   A ☐   B ☐   C ☐

3   What does Katy want for breakfast?   4   What did Frank eat at the party?

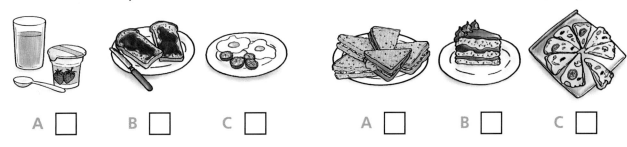

A ☐   B ☐   C ☐   A ☐   B ☐   C ☐

D **Read the sentences and write one word on each line.**

How often do you ...	never	sometimes	every day	points
1 .....do..... sport?	a	b	c	....
2 eat different .... of fruit and vegetables?	a	b	c	....
3 go .... bed very late?	a	b	c	....
4 have drinks with sugar .... them?	a	b	c	....
5 eat chocolate and sweets?	a	b	c	....
6 eat foods .... burgers, chips or sausages?	a	b	c	....
7 walk up or .... stairs when you could use a lift?	a	b	c	....
8 drink four or more glasses .... water each day?	a	b	c	....
9 forget to .... breakfast?	a	b	c	....
10 play on the computer for more .... two hours each day?	a	b	c	....

E **Now answer the questions. Draw a circle round a, b or c.**

15 What's for dinner?

A ▶ Listen and draw lines.

Paul   Anna   William   Richard

Jill   Harry   Eva   May

B Read the text. Choose the right words and write them on the lines.

Swans

Example	Swans are the largest water birds ....*in*................. the world. You often see wild swans on lakes or rivers. Most swans are white,	in of on
1	but you can .... see black swans in some countries.	1 also next too
2	Swans look lovely but be careful if one .... really near to you. If a swan	2 comes coming came
3	suddenly .... frightened, it will try to fly away and might hurt you. Swans have really strong wings!	3 feel feeling feels
4	Their necks are .... than any other birds' necks because they use them to help find	4 longest longer long
5	food in the water. In a river .... are lots of plants and insects for swans to eat!	5 here then there
6	Swans live together in pairs or families. Young swans don't usually leave their parents .... the next new babies join the family.	6 during before by
7	Some swans don't like winter weather so when it starts getting colder, ... wonderful birds begin the long journey	7 this all these
8	.... warmer environments.	8 on to at
9	Wild swans usually live for about twenty years but swans .... live in places like	9 which what who
10	zoos .... live for fifty years!	10 can would must

C Find out what Grace and Tom are doing!

D ▶ **Listen and order the pictures 1–6.**

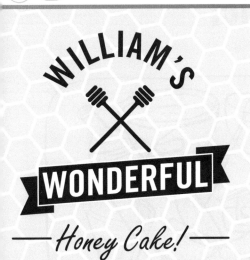

WILLIAM'S
WONDERFUL
— *Honey Cake!* —

YOU NEED:

EGGS ◯ HONEY ◯

FLOUR ◯ MILK ◯

SUGAR ◯ BUTTER ◯

LEMON ◯

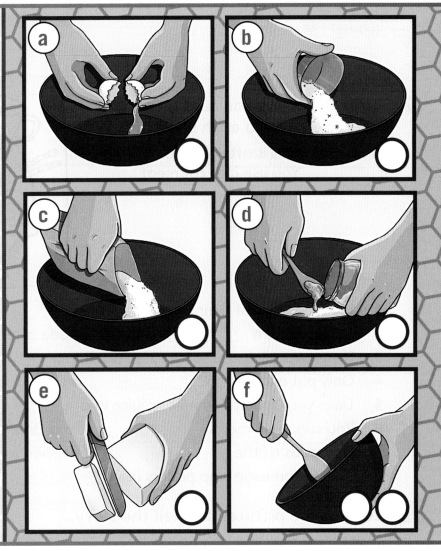

E **Write funny food sentences for all your friends!**

Mary ate all of Mum's meat at midnight on Monday!
Tom had too many tomatoes at ten o'clock on Tuesday!
William had some wonderful watermelon on Wednesday!
Tony took tea to his thirsty teacher at teatime on Thursday!
Fred had fish fingers and fries at five o'clock on Friday!

Sue .... on Saturday.

Sophia .... on Sunday.

F **Ask and answer questions.**

Let's talk about food.
What's your favourite food?

Who cooks most of the
food in your home?

Tell me about the food you
ate for dinner yesterday.

Where do you eat
at home?

35

16 Let's have a picnic!

A Write what you can see.
Add one word to each sentence.

Example: This is often made of metal.
You use it to cut meat.

...... a knife ......

1 Most people put their food on a round .... before they eat it.
2 I often have a .... of lemonade after a ride on my racing bike.
3 If you want to have some soup, put it in a ....
4 Only put a little black .... on your food because it tastes hot!
5 Does your family buy milk or juice in a .... ? Mine does.
6 You can use a metal .... to mix different kinds of food together.
7 Dad adds a little .... , not pepper, to meat when he cooks it.
8 I know someone who prefers using .... to eat rice.

B Look at the pictures and tell the story.

1

2

3

4

C **Look at the picture and read the story.**
Write words to complete the sentences. Use 1, 2, 3 or 4 words.

That is such a good idea!

Lucy West likes being an office manager, but when it's hot and sunny she looks out of the window at the view and dreams of holidays in the countryside. Last Thursday morning, the weather was wonderful. But there was so much work to do. Lucy turned on her computer and started answering lots of important emails.

At twelve o'clock she said to Alice, a designer who worked in the room as well, 'We need a holiday! But we can't leave the office. What shall we do?'

'Let's have a holiday here in our lunch break!' Alice said. 'Turn off the computers!'

The two women moved their desks and computers and put a blanket and two cushions from the office cupboard down on the floor. Alice fetched a huge plate, two glasses and a cold bottle of lemonade from the office kitchen and then took some cheese, olives and cookies from her shopping bag. Alice played a CD of wild birds singing and the warm light from the sun came through the open office window.

The women sat on the blanket, had their picnic, closed their eyes and dreamed of being in the countryside. It was difficult to start work again that afternoon! When Lucy got home her husband asked, 'Was it busy in the office today?' 'Yes! I wrote 148 emails and fixed a computer program and Alice finished her project,' she laughed. 'But we went on holiday too!'

Examples

Lucy likes her job. She's an office ....*manager*.................... .

Lucy looks out of the window when it's ....*hot and sunny*.............. outside.

Questions

1 The .... was fantastic last Thursday morning.

2 Lucy had to write lots of .... that morning.

3 A designer called .... worked in the office as well.

4 At twelve o'clock, the two women .... their computers.

5 Alice went to the office kitchen to get a ...., a plate and some glasses.

6 The women listened to .... of some birds singing.

7 Lucy wrote more than a hundred emails and she also .... that day!

D *Funtime* **Let's play a guessing game!**

17 A day's work

A Look at the pictures. Write the jobs.

```
                    7
  1 |m|  |  |  |  | |
              2 |c| |  |  |  | |
      3 |p|  | |  |  |  |  |  | |
          4 |j| |  |  |  |  |  | |
  5 |m|  |  |  | |
  6 |d|  |  |  | |
```

B Read the sentences. Write the jobs from the crossword.

1   *a photographer* This person takes pictures of interesting places and people for magazines.

2   .... This person finds out about things that happen and then writes about them for newspapers and different television channels.

3   .... This person works in an office and helps other people to work well.

4   .... This person makes delicious things for people to eat in restaurants.

5   .... You go to see these people if you are ill. If you are feeling sick or sore, they give you the right medicine.

6   .... This person can repair your car if there's a problem with its engine.

7   .... These people act on a theatre stage and people go to watch them.

C ▶ Listen and write the numbers of the job in A.

a ....   b ....   c ....   d ....

D Which of these jobs do you like best? Which is the worst? Write the jobs next to the numbers.

1 is the worst job! 8 is the best job!

| engineer   designer   police officer   shop manager   film star   dentist   firefighter   pop s⟩ |

1 ....   2 ....   3 ....   4 ....

5 ....   6 ....   7 ....   8 ....

E ▶ **What did Sarah take to each place? Listen and write a letter in each box.**

letters B

a map ☐

a scarf ☐

an umbrella ☐

a tablet ☐

a teddy bear ☐

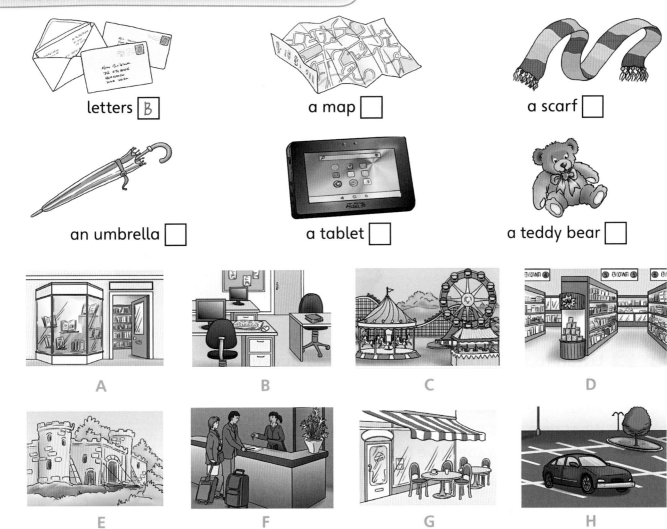

A   B   C   D

E   F   G   H

F **Look at the pictures and tell the story.**

Sarah talks to a pop star

1

Matt

Sarah

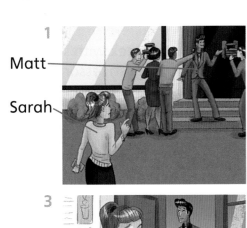

2

5

THE NEWS

OUR JOURNALIST SARAH TALKS TO MATT EAGLE

3

4

39

18 Time and work

A What's the time?

a

1
3 o'clock

b

☐
....

c

☐
....

d

☐
....

e

☐
....

f

☐
....

B ▶ Listen to the conversations and read questions 1–4.
Find the correct answers in A. Write 2, 3 and 4 in the boxes in A.

1 What time is lunch today?
2 What time does the boy's television programme begin?
3 What time does Zoe have to get up for school?
4 What time is it now?

C Read the story. Choose a word from the box.
Write the correct word next to the numbers 1–5.

Example

classmates   family   borrowing   later   art   hour   factory   skiing   fetch   use

Michael is in London. He flew there last week with some of his ...classmates... . They're having English lessons at a college in the city centre. He's talking and sending messages to the other people in his family on the internet. He does this in his afternoon lesson break.

His father, Jim, teaches (1)...................... but he's at home now. His mother, Mary, is a businesswoman. She's visiting a (2)...................... in China where they design apps and make laptops and tablets. His sister, Emma, is in another country too. She's (3)...................... with her class in the mountains!

Michael's family had to think carefully about a good time to talk to each other because the time is different in each of the four countries. Michael can (4)...................... the computer room in London at 4 p.m. Back at home, his dad turns on the computer at 7 p.m. to talk. After a day in the mountains, Emma goes online in her hotel at 5 p.m. But their conversation is much (5)...................... for Michael's mother. Where she is, it's 1 a.m!

6 Now choose the best name for this story. Tick (✔) one box.

Emma's funny day at the airport ☐

Michael's family conversation ☐

A lesson for Michael's dad ☐

D ▶ Listen and tick (✔) the box.

Example   What's Kim's job?   1   How does Kim go to work?

A ✔   B ☐   C ☐   A ☐   B ☐   C ☐

2   What time does Kim start work?   3   Where does Kim have lunch?

A ☐   B ☐   C ☐   A ☐   B ☐   C ☐

4   What was Kim's first job?   5   What does Kim like most about
                                                    her job?

A ☐   B ☐   C ☐   A ☐   B ☐   C ☐

E Funtime Play the game! Which job have I drawn?

19 Answer my questions

A Read the story. Choose a word from the box.
Write the correct word next to numbers 1–5.

Example

light   candy   hear   decide   project   asleep   building   explore   hurry   scary

Daisy Brown had a little brother called Hugo who made her angry! Hugo was only
five but he never, never stopped asking questions! 'How does a ...._light_........ turn
on and off, Daisy? How long is a dinosaur's tail, Aunt Sally? Why can dogs' ears
(1) .... some noises that I can't, Grandpa?'

He sometimes asked really difficult questions. 'What's in the middle of our planet,
Mum? Why are jellyfish so (2) ...., Grandma? Why do frogs live in ponds,
Dad? Why have tigers got striped bodies, Daisy?' People usually said, 'I don't know,
Hugo!'

One day, while Dad, Daisy and Hugo were walking along a street in the city
centre Hugo pointed to an enormous new (3) .... and asked, 'What's inside
that, Daisy?' Daisy didn't know, but their father did. 'It's a science museum. Let's go
inside!'

'Fantastic! I can get some ideas for my next science (4) .... at school, too.'
said Daisy and then turned to Hugo. 'What shall we (5) .... first?' That was
a difficult question for Hugo. 'I don't know!' he said!

6   Now choose the best name for the story. Tick one box.

Daisy's favourite pets ☐

Answers for Hugo ☐

Dad's trip to town ☐

B ▶ **Listen and colour the museum picture in A.**

C Write the correct question words after numbers 1–12. Ask your friends the questions!

How many   How much   How often   How old   What
What time   When   ~~Where~~   Which   Who   Whose   Why   How

	Your name ....
Name	Example ......Where...... do you live?
....	1 .... is your surname?
....	2 .... is the cleverest student in this class?
....	3 .... did you come to school today? Did you cycle?
....	4 .... birthday is in April?
....	5 .... are you? 10? 11?
....	6 .... did you get up this morning? Seven o'clock?
....	7 .... work do you do on a tablet, laptop or computer? Too much?
....	8 .... people live in your house? Four? Five?
....	9 .... is the best place to go? A museum, a funfair or a music festival?
....	10 .... do you use apps? Every day?
....	11 .... will you go home? Soon?
....	12 .... are you learning English?

D Write questions! Answer questions!

on the beach

1 .... ?

in class

2 .... ?

3 .... ?

in a museum

4 .... ?

at a party

E *Funtime* Play the game! Questions mingle.

20 Calling and sending

A What has Charlie lost?

B Read the story. Choose words from the phone. Write the correct words next to numbers 1–5.

When Charlie got back home after his school trip to Hardhill Castle, he put everything that was in his backpack on the dining room table. 'Where's my phone?' he said. 'I was ....sure........ it was in here.' He suddenly began to feel really worried! 'That's a surprise!' he thought. 'Oh no! It's (1) .... ! I hope it didn't fall out through this hole!'

'What am I going to do? I can't (2) ....
Holly or text her, so she'll be really angry with me.
I can't go (3) .... to read Grandma's email again or do the searches I need for my history homework. I have to look at that (4) ....
about important explorers who went on sea journeys in the nineteenth century. There's also that brilliant new e-book that Michael told me about. It's so exciting! I wanted to read that this evening.'

And then he thought: 'What's that noise? It
(5) .... like my phone! So where is it? Oh! It's in my trouser pocket!' Charlie took it out, looked at the screen to see who was phoning him and said, 'Oh! Hurray! It's you Holly! Sorry about yesterday ...'

sounds
instrument
~~sure~~ call
ONLINE
strange
repeats
wifi
MISSING
WEBSITE

6 Choose words to make the best name for the story.

Holly	changes		finds		headteacher.
Charlie	turns on	then	sends	his	rucksack.
Mrs Hope	loses		repairs	her	phone.

C **When did these things happen? Write years.**

1 Martin Cooper had the first mobile phone conversation.

....

2 Shops sold the first mobile with an address book, email and calendar.

....

3 You could only save 30 phone numbers on your phone.

....

4  First phone with a camera.

....

5 British engineer Neil Papworth sent the first SMS (text message).

....

6 The first phone with internet.

....

7 You could pay for things in shops with your phone.

....

8 The first phone with a game.

....

1973   1983   1992   1993   1994   1998   1999   2000   2011

In ....

D **Ask and answer questions about Eva and Robert's phones.**

Eva's new phone	
When/get	?
Colour	?
Big/small screen	?
Who/often call	?
Where/keep	?
How many messages/ send each day	?
How many tunes/ listen to each day	?

E *Funtime* **Play the game! The verb–noun chain.**

21 The time of the year

A How many words can you find on the calendar page?

September

1 fall	2	3 a week	4 hours	5	6	7 midnight
8	9 summer	10	11 a weekend	12	13	14 a year
15	16 midday	17 days	18	19	20 a century	21
22 months	23	24	25 minutes	26	27 a diary	28 winter
29	30 at the moment					

Write the blue words on the line:

shortest time > minutes, ...

.... > longest time

B Choose words from the calendar in A and write them on the lines.

Example   There are usually 365 days in this. ....a year.........

1   In some parts of the world, this means 'autumn'. ....

2   The weather at this time of the year is the warmest. ....

3   This is another way of saying 12.00 in the afternoon. ....

4   In each hour, there are 60 of these. ....

5   Most people are awake for about 16 of these each day. ....

6   This is another way to say Saturday and Sunday. ....

7   You can see the names of 12 of these on any calendar. ....

8   A new one of these begins every hundred years. ....

9   This is usually the coldest and darkest time of the year. ....

10   This is when one day finishes and another begins. ....

11   This is another way to say 'now'. ....

C Put the words in the spring, summer, autumn or winter boxes.

> baby animals   making a snowman   going on a beach holiday
> birds making nests   ice skating   leaves falling   camping   starting school   cold
> wet   finishing school   flies   first flowers appearing   hot   skiing   warm
> picnics   soup   bears going to sleep   January   April   December   July   August
> February   March   June   September   May   November   October

spring	....
	....
summer	....
	....
autumn (fall)	....
	....
winter	cold ....
	....

D Look at the pictures. What differences can you see?

A

B

E Read the message and write the missing words.
Write one word on each line.

Example	Uncle George is amazing! This afternoon, he drove me ..... *to* .....
1	Appletree Forest where I met two .... my friends,
2	Julia and Mark. They cycled there today on their new ....
	First, we made boats from an old newspaper and then sailed
3	.... best one down the stream. It's not deep there. The boat
4	moved fast because it .... quite windy today. After that, we
	went fishing. We were lucky as well! We caught four fish!
5	Uncle George .... a fire from some wood so we could cook
	the fish for our lunch.
	We all had a really wonderful time.

F *Funtime* Play time games!

22 Important numbers

A How long / tall / high / far away? Match the drawings and numbers.

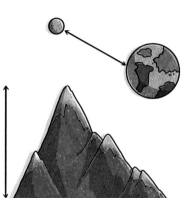

384,403 km

32 cm

8 m

1.70 m

2,616 m

B Tick (✔) the pictures of the people you read about.

Example	**The youngest and the oldest**
	Here's some interesting information. Did
	you ......_know_...... that the youngest
	driver in the world passed his driving test
1	.... 27 March 1974 when he was
	14 years 235 days old!
2	The youngest golfer to hit a golf ball all the way to the flag .... called Matthew Draper. Matthew hit the ball 112
3	metres .... he was only 5 years
4	212 days old when he .... that!
5	Sydney Ling was only 13 when he wrote, ... also filmed, the famous movie, 'Lex the Wonderdog', in 1973. The
6	film was 92 minutes ....!
7	Harry Stevens was the oldest person in the world to get married when he became a new husband at the age .... 103! His
8	new wife was .... 84!
9	The oldest person to fly in a plane was Charlotte Hughes. .... gave her a passenger ticket for her 110th birthday. It was to fly from London to New York but actually, that wasn't the last time she
10	.... in a plane! She travelled by air again when she was 115! What a fantastic adventure for her!

C Choose the right words and write them on the lines in B.

Example	know	knew	knowing				
1	in	on	at	6	long	longer	longest
2	be	were	was	7	with	by	of
3	but	or	if	8	instead	after	already
4	doing	does	did	9	Someone	No-one	Anyone
5	because	and	after	10	flies	flew	flying

D ▶ Listen and write.

Tamae Watanabe

1 Climbed: ....
2 Age the first time: ....
3 Date of second time: May ...., 2012
4 Time they got to the top: .... a.m.
5 Mountain is: .... metres high

E Complete the sentences with your numbers!

I'm .... metres tall.

My lucky number is ....

My birthday is on ....

My telephone number is ....

I think I know .... English words!

I often travel on the number .... bus.

It takes me .... minutes to come to school.

My school is .... kilometres from my house.

About .... people live in the village/town/city where my home is.

And today, I am ☐ years ☐ months and ☐ days old!

F Do the birthday puzzle!

PROJECT

49

23 World, weather, work

Look and read. Choose the correct words and write them on the lines.

wifi

ice

fog

an office

a dentist

a cave

a pop star

the sky

	Businessmen and businesswomen go to this place to work and have meetings.	*an office*
1	When you are online, you can find all kinds of information on these.	....
2	This person can fix a tooth that has a hole in it.	....
3	If you visit this very dark place in the rocks, you might see bats inside it.	....
4	You might feel frightened in this loud, wet and windy kind of weather.	....
5	You might see this person sing or play an instrument on TV.	....
6	In this kind of weather, it's very difficult to see places that are far away.	....
7	Only plants that don't need lots of water can grow in this hot, dry place.	....
8	You look at words and pictures on this part of a computer when you're studying.	....
9	Look up when you are outside in the day or at night and you will always see this.	....
10	This is sea water that moves up and down in the wind.	....

a desert

a wave

a storm

the land

a designer

a screen

websites

B **Add information to Mr Wild's business email! You choose!**

Good morning, Dan!
Thanks for your message. Actually, I've got an engineers' *meeting* at 9.30 and after that I need to add some important information about our (1) ....
to the website, but I can meet you at (2) .... Is that OK with you? Come
to my (3) .... I want to hear all about your trip to the (4) ....
factory! I also want to show you the photos of the (5) .... that we're
going to put in the (6) .... next month. Please bring the (7) ....
to our meeting. I want to look at those, too.
I've got to collect some (8) .... tickets in the lunch break so I'm sorry I
can't join you for lunch! Enjoy your (9) .... ! It always tastes so good!

I had problems with my car engine this morning so had to get a (10) .... into town. I think it's going to (11) .... later so can you give me a lift home this afternoon? I live in Stone Street which is very near the (12) .... I've got to hurry to the meeting now.

See you later, Richard Wild

C Look at the three pictures. Write about this story. Write 20 or more words.

D Two words or one word?

there's ... I've ... who's ... we're ...

E Funtime Play the game. The verb–noun chain!

24 Leaving and arriving

A Choose two words to complete each sentence.

> platform   path   love   countries   ride   sky   visit   ~~pilot~~   catch   planets
> passenger   city   wheels   ticket   journey   astronauts   airport   ~~fly~~

Example   A ....pilot........ sometimes uses a helicopter to ....fly......... to
people who are in danger or need someone to help them very quickly.

1 You have to wait on the .... at a railway station if you want to
.... a train.

2 Sometimes .... travel into space in rockets to find out more about
science and other ....

3 A .... has to pay a taxi driver quite a lot of money to take them
from one part of the .... to another.

4 When you go for a .... on a bicycle, you use your feet to make
its .... turn round and round!

5 In many .... you need to buy a .... before you can
travel on a bus or train.

6 People need to get on a plane at an .... to go on a long
.... by air.

7 People who .... adventures might go for rides in hot air balloons
high up in the .... !

B ▶ Listen to the sentences about picture 1. How is picture 2 different?

Example   In my picture, the man on the motorbike has got a red bag.

1

2

C Draw lines between words that mean the same.

1 **Travelling** to London takes three hours.
2 Mum **drove me** to the city centre.
3 Grandma **took** the wrong bus!
4 I **rode my bike** to school last week.
5 We **crossed** the desert **on foot**.
6 We **arrived at** the airport at six thirty.
7 My parents **flew** to the holiday island.

A gave me a lift
B caught
C walked across
D went by helicopter
E trips
F The journey
G cycled
H got to

D ▶ How did Uncle Oliver get to each place?
Listen and write a letter (A–H) in each box.

A

B

.... G .... ☐

C

D

.... ☐ .... ☐

E

F

.... ☐ .... ☐

G

H

E Answer Peter's questions about Uncle Oliver. What does Sophia say?
Write 1, 2, 3 or 4 words.

1 Peter: Why did your uncle go to the airport?
Sophia: He went there to meet _an important person_ .

2 Peter: What's the quickest way to get to the museum?
Sophia: Going to the museum .... is the quickest.

3 Peter: Where did your uncle lose his money?
Sophia: He dropped it in the .... when he was riding there on his bike.

4 Peter: Did your uncle enjoy his ride in the helicopter?
Sophia: Of course he did! It was a .... day because he was so high in the air.

5 Peter: Did your uncle go to any places which weren't for work?
Sophia: Yes. He went to a restaurant one evening by .... It's his favourite place to eat.

25 What shall we do next?

A Read about Clare and Matt in the museum.

Clare and Matt are on their school trip. They're in a really interesting computer science museum. They're sitting at a large table where there are three computers and lots of other things to look at. Clare and Matt are playing a science game on two of the computers. Their teacher is watching them. Clare and Matt aren't alone. Quite a lot of other children are in the same part of the museum. They're looking at something on the wall.

Imagine a picture of Clare and Matt in the museum and answer the questions.

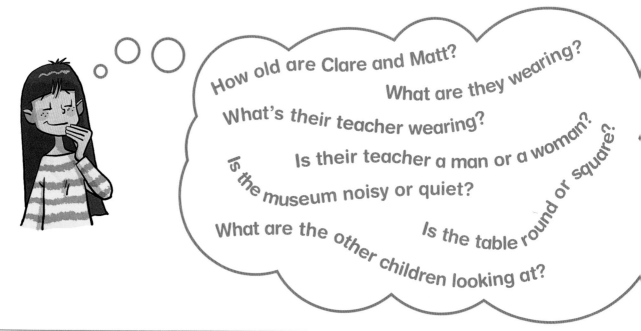

How old are Clare and Matt?

What are they wearing?

What's their teacher wearing?

Is their teacher a man or a woman?

Is the museum noisy or quiet?

Is the table round or square?

What are the other children looking at?

B Ask and answer questions about two school trips.

C ▶ Listen and write ten things to take on a trip.

D ▶ Listen and write yes or no.

1 ...yes...   2 ....
3 ....   4 ....
5 ....   6 ....
7 ....   8 ....

E Look at the picture and read the story.

Mary's naughty friend

Mary felt too excited to eat her dinner. She suddenly jumped up from the table and said, 'I'm going to phone Grandma before I go on my school trip!'

Mary's grandmother was surprised to hear her granddaughter on the phone. 'It's quite late, Mary.' 'I know, but I'm so excited,' Mary answered. 'I'm going to go on a school camping holiday. My friends and I are going to have lots of fun!' 'Wow!' her grandmother said.

'We have to take pens and write about the birds there. Perhaps bears, too!' Mary said. 'And my friend and I are going to look for a big, dark cave with wild bats and huge furry mountain monsters inside! We don't get frightened by things like that!'

'Well, it sounds scary to me,' Grandma laughed. 'But you're brave! Tell me more!' 'Well, we have to take things for washing,' Mary answered. 'But my friend and I are going to wash outside. We can clean our dirty faces in the rain! And we have to take things for eating, like forks and spoons, but my friend and I are going to put sweets and chocolate biscuits in our rucksacks too, so we can have midnight snacks. And we're going to put beetles in Nick White's trainers and spiders in his bed!'

'Who's this naughty friend of yours, Mary?' Grandma asked. 'I'm not going to tell you that, Grandma,' Mary answered. 'It's a secret!'

F Write some words to complete the sentences.
You can use 1, 2, 3 or 4 words.

Examples   Mary couldn't ....*eat her dinner*.... because she was too excited.
              She left the table and went to phone her ....*grandma*........ .

Questions

1 Mary's grandma felt .... when Mary phoned her.

2 Mary and her friends are going to have fun on their ....

3 Mary and her friend want to find wild bats and .... in the cave.

4 Grandma thinks Mary is ....

5 Mary says that they're going to wash .... in the rain!

6 Mary and her friend are going to eat .... in the night.

7 Mary doesn't say the name of her friend because that's a ....

G 🅵🆄🅽🆃🅸🅼🅴 Play the game. Topic words!

26 Where can we go on holiday?

A Match four of the word circles with the pictures.

tentcampingtorch   rucksackclimbingsky   sailingview island   city hotel entrance   wild animals jungle adventure

B Complete the holiday diary. Write one word in each space.

I spent most ......of...... this morning in the pool but in (1) .... afternoon, Dad drove us to a city (2) .... was quite far away. I thought that (3) .... quite boring. After dinner, we (4) .... down in a circle round a fire and told stories. One was (5) .... a person who lived in the mountains and found an eagle's nest! We went to bed really late. Sleeping (6) .... the ground isn't easy! It's quite cold (7) .... hard. But camping is much more fun than staying (8) .... a hotel!

C Read the conversation and choose the best answer (A–H).

Example

Ben: This is our last week of school before the holidays!

Helen: ....C.....

1 Ben: Where do you usually go on holiday?
   Helen: ....
2 Ben: Do you stay in a hotel?
   Helen: ....
3 Ben: What do you have to take with you on holiday, then?
   Helen: ....
4 Ben: What do you do during the day?
   Helen: ....
5 Ben: This year, we're going to go to London. Have you been there?
   Helen: ....

A   No. A science tour two years ago.
B   What a big building!
C   I know. It's brilliant, isn't it! We're going to go away. Example
D   We love looking for wild animals!
E   Lots of things, like blankets and torches.
F   No, in a tent. We prefer doing that.
G   To the mountains like you did last year.
H   No! You're so lucky! Can I come too?

D Look at the pictures and tell the story.

The day we forgot our tent

Helen

Robert

E ▶ Listen and colour and write.

27 It's the holidays! Bye!

A **Make a story with the seven pictures.**

B **Read the story. Choose a word from the box.**
Write the correct word next to the numbers 1–5.

> **Example**
>
> beach   touch   wonderful   missing   hid   unkind   strawberries
> collecting   cave   watering

Every summer, Jim goes to the ......beach...... with his parents and two cousins, Emma and Alice. One afternoon they all sailed to a little island. They took some cheese sandwiches, salad and (1) .... and ate their picnic on some rocks next to a small stream.

Then Emma said to Jim and Alice, 'Let's go for a walk along the sand. We might find something really exciting there.' 'Cool!' said Alice and Jim. They found a big dark (2) .... where the waves went in and out. 'Perhaps an enormous octopus or a scary jellyfish lives in here!' Jim whispered. Emma laughed. 'Or perhaps pirates came in a huge ship and (3) .... their gold and silver treasure here!' she said. The children spent a long time (4) .... shells from deep between the rocks there. When they were getting ready to leave, a man suddenly appeared in the entrance. He was wearing black boots and looked very tall. 'Oh no! It's a pirate!' Sarah said.

'Don't worry! It's me!' Jim's dad called. 'Wow! What a (5) .... place! But come on! It's time to go home!'

6 **Now choose the best name for the story. Tick (✔) one box.**

Our sailing game ☐

Fun on the island ☐

The pirate family ☐

C ▶ **Listen! What's Lily going to do today? Tick (✔) the boxes.**

play chess ☐   eat lots of biscuits ☐

watch a TV programme ☐   go on a journey ☐

repair her bicycle ☐   write messages ☐

join a club ☐   be really lazy! ☐

play video games ☐

read an adventure story ☐

D **Decide what you are going to do tomorrow!**
Complete the sentences.

Tomorrow is the first day of my holidays!
I'm not going to get up until ....
I'm going to have .... for breakfast.
Then I'm going to put on my .... and
call my friend whose name is .... because
....
While I'm having lunch I'm going to ....
Then I'm going to go to .... and then I'm going
to ....
After having my favourite dinner which is .... ,
I'm going to ....
And I'm not going to go to bed until ....!
See you!
Bye for now. 🙂

E *Funtime* **Play the game. Really?**

59

28 I want to win!

A **What was each person doing? Read and write names.**

At twenty-five to six, who:

Example   was moving one of the chess pieces?   ....Holly.......

1   was feeling worried about the game?   ....

2   was lifting something above people's heads?   ....

3   was explaining the game to the others?   ....

4   was hoping he might win soon?   ....

5   was sending someone a message?   ....

6   was thinking about the next meal?   ....

B **Look at the picture in A.**
Answer the questions then write the story.

Are all these children classmates?

What were they doing before this? Gym? Science? Maths?

Are they in a chess club or is this part of a lesson?

What time of day is it?

Is it a competition? Did everyone play?

What happened at the end of the game?

C Read Paul's text message. Write the missing words.

Hi Kim! I can't believe it! I won the adventure story competition! I wrote ....*about*.... a boy who got lost in the rain forest. I won a great (1) .... It's tickets for me, a friend and my family to go to the new funfair, the one (2) .... is near Henley Stadium. We'll go on Saturday. (3) .... you like to come with us? Dad can (4) .... us all there in our car. It's an amazing place with (5) .... of frightening rides! Ask your mum and then tell me at school tomorrow.
See you!
Paul

D ▶ Anna's competition. Listen and tick (✔) the box.

What kind of competition is Anna getting ready for?

A ☐   B ☐   C ✔

1 Who is helping Anna?

A ☐   B ☐   C ☐

2 What is the date of the competition?

A ☐   B ☐   C ☐

3 How did Anna find out about the competition?

A ☐   B ☐   C ☐

4 What is the first prize?

A ☐   B ☐   C ☐

5 Where is Anna going to go now?

A ☐   B ☐   C ☐

E Funtime Play the word game! How many new *Flyers* words can you make?

An adventure story competition

29 Doing sport! Having fun!

A ▶ **Write twelve things you can see in the picture.**

snow
....

....

B ▶ **Listen and draw lines.**

Vicky   Frank   Hugo   Tom

Alex   Eva   Jill

C **Write answers.**

Which girl is Jill? Where is she? How old is she? What is she wearing?
What is she doing? How is she feeling? Is she having fun?

....

....

....

D Write the answers to the sports quiz.

1   When people do this sport, they stand or sit and try to catch
    something that lives in the water. They might eat it later!   ....

2   Five players bounce and throw the ball in this sport.
    Teams wear special shorts and T-shirts in different colours.   ....

3   You wear special boots and move quickly down snow in this
    popular sport. One foot is always behind the other.   ....

4   You can try to win alone or with your partner in this sport.
    You use a round bat to hit a small ball across a table.   ....

5   When we do this sport, we use our arms and legs to push
    our bodies through the water.   ....

6   In this sport, you practise hitting a very small ball and try
    to make it fall down a hole that's got a flag in it.   ....

7   People do this sport on ice. It looks like dancing sometimes!   ....

8   When we play this, we hit the ball in the air with our hands
    or arms. We don't want the ball to fall on the ground!   ....

9   Sometimes people race in boats in this sport. It is usually a safe
    sport but might be quite dangerous if the wind is strong.   ....

10 In this sport, players hit a hard ball across the grass or across
    ice. The team that scores the most goals are the winners!   ....

E Look at the pictures in B and E. What differences can you see?

F ▶ Listen and write your answers.

30 Summer and winter sports

A Which person won the bike race?

The person who won wore red gloves ...

... and shorts without pockets ...

... and forgot their sunglasses ...

... and wore a helmet with stripes ...

... and their bike had black stripes on it.

... and their wheels looked quite unusual ...

B Write to, because, while or so.

1 Holly and I went to the mountains last weekend ....*because*........ we love snow sports.

2 Holly can't ski .... she took her sledge instead.

3 It was funny! Holly fell over in the snow .... she was chatting on her phone!

4 We took our ice skates as well .... you can skate on the lake there.

5 After some delicious hot chocolate, Holly got ready .... do something silly!

6 I skated around the lake .... Holly was making her snowman.

7 Holly wanted to have some more fun .... she decided to throw snowballs at me!

8 I put on my skis .... I wanted more practice and skied by myself for an hour.

C **Read the story and write answers. You can use 1, 2, 3 or 4 words.**

The wrong suitcase!

Lucy and her parents, Mr and Mrs Field, put their summer clothes and swimming and sailing things in their big, blue suitcase and drove to the airport. Lucy was excited because she was going on a sports holiday. When they got to the airport, Lucy's dad showed their tickets and then the family hurried to the bookshop to choose some magazines.

After that, they went to get on the plane. Lucy's seat was by the window! During the journey, Lucy's mum read about a famous ice hockey team, her dad talked to another passenger about a golf match and Lucy watched an adventure film about mountain climbing. When they got off the plane, they took a taxi to the hotel. 'Wow!' said Lucy when they arrived. 'Look at all the sailing boats! And, look! You can play table tennis by the pool. Oh! Where's my swimsuit? Can I go for a swim? I can't wait until tomorrow!'

'Not yet, Lucy,' her mother said. 'We have to take our things up to our room first.' When Lucy's father picked up the suitcase, he said, 'That's strange. This feels much heavier than it did before!'

Mrs Field laughed. 'You think that because you're tired after our long journey! Come on! I've got our key. Look! Our room number is 501. It's on the fifth floor.' They went up in the lift, found their room and went inside. Then Lucy's dad opened the suitcase to take out their swimming things. 'Oh no!' he said. 'Whose ski hat is this? Why are there three pairs of gloves and all these warm socks in the suitcase?'

What a terrible mistake! The family had the wrong suitcase!

Examples

The Field family put all their holiday things in a .....big, blue suitcase...... .

Lucy was feeling really ....excited............ about going on a sports holiday.

Questions

1   Before they got on the plane, the family bought .... from a shop.

2   On the plane, Lucy's mum read about some famous .... players and her father talked about golf.

3   The adventure film that Lucy saw was about ....

4   Lucy wanted to .... when they arrived at the hotel.

5   They went up in the lift because their room was on .... floor.

6   .... opened the suitcase to get out the swimming things.

7   Inside the suitcase, they found a hat, ... and some warm socks!

D **Look at the pictures and tell the story.**

E 🄵🅄🄽🅃🄸🄼🄴 **Play the game. Why?**

31 Here and there

A Match the pictures with the sentences. Write the correct letter in each square.

1   2   3   4   5

A   Zoe showed her new skateboard to her friends at the skatepark yesterday.
B   My uncle played the drums in this year's summer music festival.
C   Dan's interested in really unusual creatures that live deep in the ocean.
D   One of the rides at the funfair was silly, but most of them were great.
E   People come to this place to choose something really delicious to eat.
F   We went on a school trip to the stadium to meet our city's football team.

B Look at the three pictures. Write about this story. Write 20 or more words.

C Find 5 differences between the skatepark pictures.

D Aunt Zoe is talking to Robert in a café in the museum. What does Robert say?

Example   Aunt Zoe: What a nice café this is in the museum.

        Robert: ....B........

1   Aunt Zoe: Shall we sit over there, next to the door?
   Robert: ....
2   Aunt Zoe: What would you like to eat and drink?
   Robert: ....
3   Aunt Zoe: Have you been here before?
   Robert: ....
4   Aunt Zoe: Which part of the museum did you enjoy most?
   Robert: ....
5   Aunt Zoe: What would you like to do next?
   Robert: ....
   Aunt Zoe: Alright.

A   When everyone clapped at the end of the video.
B   Yes! It's really cool. I enjoyed the museum very much, too.   Example
C   By the window is better, I think.
D   Where they've got all those posters of sports cars.
E   A pancake and a banana milkshake if they have those here.
F   Can we buy that poster about fixing engines from the museum shop?
G   No. It's as important as learning English.
H   Only once. On last year's school trip, remember?

32 Where?

A Write the names under the things.

B

....

....

....

....

....

....

B ▶ Where did Jack take each thing? Listen and write a letter (A–H) in each box.

A

B

C

D

E

F

G

H

C Read the text. Choose the right words and write them on the lines.

Buildings

Example Thousands of years ......*ago*......, people didn't stay in the same place because they

1 had to travel .... find food. They
2 lived in caves or slept in tents .... were made from animal fur. They cooked their food on fires that also kept them warm
3 .... the long, cold and wet winters.
4 Fires kept people safe too .... wild animals are afraid of fire.

5 Our homes .... changed a lot since then! Most people now live in warm, dry and safe buildings.

In some big cities you can find new buildings
6 that might have more .... a hundred floors. These are called skyscrapers.

Some skyscrapers have gardens on
7 .... roofs. You can make a 'green roof' by planting different kinds
8 .... grass there. On some city buildings, you can also see 'green walls'.

9 In big cities, ... green roofs and walls is a really good idea. The leaves on the plants help clean the air and make our
10 environment much ....

	since	for	ago
1	for	to	with
2	which	what	who
3	during	past	until
4	so	because	before
5	have	are	do
6	when	than	if
7	theirs	its	their
8	off	from	of
9	making	made	makes
10	better	good	best

D Look and describe. What is unusual about these homes?

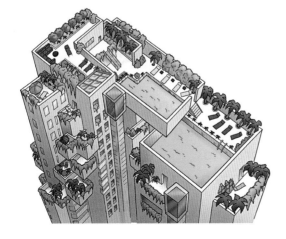

33 At the hospital

A Read the sentences and find the answers in the box.

Example When you have one of these, you might have a cough and your nose goes red!

1 Someone will drive you really quickly to this place if you are suddenly very ill.
2 You go to see this person if one of your teeth breaks or hurts badly.
3 If you feel sick, the doctor might give you some of this to help you feel better.
4 You can buy something here for a headache. This place sells things like soap, shampoo and combs as well.
5 These people look after anyone who has to stay in hospital because they are ill.
6 This is often white with a blue light on its roof and you can travel quickly to hospital in it.

a	h	o	s	p	i	t	a	l	t	a
t	e	m	p	e	r	a	t	u	r	e
p	a	c	h	e	m	i	s	t	s	m
a	n	a	m	b	u	l	a	n	c	e
n	r	f	e	r	c	l	c	h	r	d
u	u	g	a	o	k	m	o	u	y	i
r	q	v	w	k	y	o	l	r	b	c
s	i	j	x	e	b	z	d	t	d	i
e	a	d	e	n	t	i	s	t	i	n
s	t	o	m	a	c	h	a	c	h	e

B ▶ Listen and draw lines.

Michael

Mark

Katy

William

Betty

Sarah

Mary

C Complete the sentences with names and other words from the box in A.

1 .... , the girl in the striped T-shirt, has got a .... leg.
2 .... , the boy in the white shorts, has .... his arm.
3 .... , the boy in the red jacket, has got a ....
4 .... , the girl in the purple trousers, might have a ....
5 .... , the little girl in the white T-shirt, has begun to ....

D **Read the conversation and choose the best answer.**

Example
Doctor King: Good morning, William. I'm Doctor King. What's the matter?
William: .... H ....
1   Doctor King: When did you start to feel ill?
    William: ....
2   Doctor King: Tell me what you ate yesterday evening.
    William: ....
3   Doctor King: Did the nurse take your temperature?
    William: ....
4   Doctor King: Great! Take this medicine twice a day until you feel better.
    William: ....
5   Doctor King: No, it doesn't. Now, don't have more than one pancake
                    in future! OK?
    William: ....

A   Fish, then four pancakes and a large apple pie.
B   It really hurt when I woke up this morning.
C   Sure! I don't want to feel as sick as this again!
D   If you want. But some kids helped me fix it.
E   Yes. She said it was fine.
F   I started practising when I was about five.
G   OK. Does it taste nice?
H   I've got a terrible stomach-ache. Example

E **Ask and answer questions about Doctor King and Mrs Ring's jobs.**

Job?	Doctor
When/work?	every night
Name/hospital?	Sky hospital
Where/hospital?	Station Road
New/old?	new

Job?	Ambulance driver
When/work?	each weekend
Name/hospital?	Swan hospital
Where/hospital?	Park Square
New/old?	old

34 Oliver goes to hospital

A Look at the picture and read the story. Write some words to complete the sentences about the story. You can use 1, 2, 3 or 4 words.

Last December, it didn't stop snowing. One day, Oliver and his friends went sledging on a high hill. When Oliver's sledge hit some stones, he fell and hurt his elbow and broke his leg! His friends were very worried and quickly rang Oliver's parents. His father came to help and an ambulance took Oliver to hospital.

Oliver had to stay in hospital for a few days. The nurses were friendly and kind so, at first, Oliver didn't mind. He didn't have to go to school or do any homework like his classmates. He just lay in bed in his pyjamas, and listened to pop music, played chess on his phone and watched his favourite football team scoring lots of goals on TV. But after two days, Oliver began to feel quite bored and a little unhappy.

But, on the third morning, Peter Windows, one of the players in the football team arrived! He brought Oliver a present – a pair of really cool football boots! Oliver's best friend came, too. 'You can borrow my laptop while you're here,' he said.

That afternoon, Oliver had another surprise. His teacher appeared! He brought something for Oliver as well but it was some maths homework! 'I'm sorry about your poor leg, Oliver,' he said, 'but make sure you do this before you come back to school in January!'

Examples

A lot of snow fell last .... December ....
Oliver hurt his elbow and leg when he was sledging on .... a high hill .... with his friends.

Questions

1   Oliver travelled to hospital in ....
2   Oliver liked the nurses because they were ....
3   Oliver had his phone in hospital, so he could play .... on it.
4   Oliver was bored and felt .... after two days.
5   Then a football player came and gave Oliver some ....
6   .... brought Oliver a laptop as well.
7   On the same day, Oliver's teacher gave him some .... to do as well!

B ▶ **Listen to the story. Draw lines under the differences.**

C **Read and write the missing words. Write one word on each line.**

Friday

Example | I didn't have ....*to*............ go to school again today because I'm still here in hospital. But I have
1 | made lots .... new friends here and the nurses make us all laugh.
2 | At about a half .... four, the nicest nurse came into my room and turned
3 | .... the TV because the football match was starting. Our team won, two goals to one!
4 | Dinner was OK too. We .... meatballs, tomato sauce and chips! And Mum brought me a great present. It's the new soccer
5 | game. I played .... all evening.

D ▶ **Listen and write.**

Example | Give Oliver: | his ....*art*........ book
| **Tell him**
1 | Class is learning about 20th century: | ....
2 | Read page number: | ....
3 | Artist's surname: | ....
4 | Colour of answer book: | ....
5 | Day of trip to stadium: | ....

E *Funtime* **Play the game! Put words together.**

35 What's it made of?

A **What's this? Write the words on the lines.**

Example
We use this to make small things like keys and big things like bridges because it's very strong. ....metal..........

1 This comes from trees. It's hard but you can cut it and make things like shelves or bookcases with it. ....

2 This comes from animals like sheep. Rugs and warm clothes like scarves and sweaters are made with it. ....

3 You can write or draw on pieces of this. It's usually made from trees and is flat and often white. ....

4 Expensive rings, necklaces and bracelets are sometimes made of this. Crowns too! ....

5 You can see through this so we use it to make things like windows, but did you know it's made from sand? ....

B **What can you see?**

C **Put them in the boxes!**

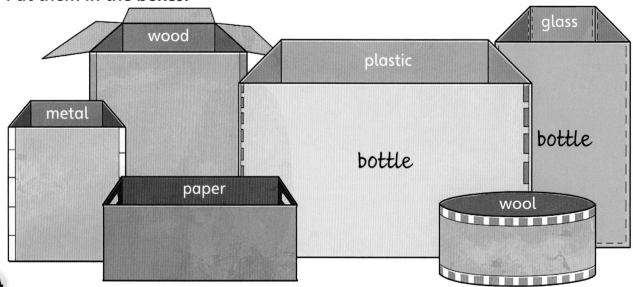

D William's and Sam's secret things. What are they made of? Tell me!

E ▶ Listen and colour and write.

F Read about glass. Choose the right words and write them on the lines.

Glass isn't new. People were making glass bowls and bottles more ....*than*........ 5,000
1 years ...., actually. But no one has ever found out who made glass first, or
2 when and where that ....

3 One story tells .... that some men from a ship arrived on a beach and decided
4 to make a meal. They made a fire on the sand and .... some small rocks
5 and stones in the middle of the fire to cook on. The fire burned .... a very
long time and the rocks and stones got really hot. Parts of the rock and some of the
6 stones began .... with the sand to make glass!

7 So .... next time you look through a window, look at a mirror
8 .... are holding a glass of water, think, 'Wow! This glass is made
from very, very hot sand!'

Example	then	than	when
1	ago	after	already
2	happen	happens	happened
3	them	us	him
4	put	puts	putting

5	from	for	off
6	mixed	mixing	mix
7	the	a	any
8	or	because	if

G Funtime Play the game! Find things in this room.

75

36 Silver, plastic, glass, gold

A **Read the clues and write the missing video game words.**

Hi Peter. Here's how you play ....

Open the first door. (1) .... the tree to find the silver key. Carry the key carefully back down the tree and put it in the plastic bag which you'll find in the metal box. Carry the key and the bag up the stairs. Take out the key and use it to open the (2) .... door. Leave the key in the door and go back down the stairs. Don't (3) .... to take the plastic bag with you.

Put the plastic bag in the tree. Now find the special rock. It's between the two lizards. Pick this up and put the rock in the metal box. Carry the box up the stairs and go through the open second door and use the rock to (4) .... the glass door. Put the box and the rock down and jump carefully through this third door. Turn on the light. In front of you is another box. This one is made of wood. The gold ring is (5) .... it. Pick the box up, run down the other stairs and throw the box on the fire. The wood will burn and then the fire will stop. You'll see the gold ring! But a monster will try to stop you picking it up. Run (6) .... back upstairs, fetch the special rock, run downstairs again and give it to the monster. The monster will go back into the cave and then you can take the gold ring!

1 means 'go up' using your hands, arms and legs (5 letters)
2 not the first, not the third, the one between the two (6 letters)
3 the opposite of 'remember' (6 letters)
4 the past of this is 'broke' (5 letters)
5 means 'in' (6 letters)
6 the opposite of 'slowly' (7 letters)

B **Look at pictures 1 and 2. Find six differences.**

1

2

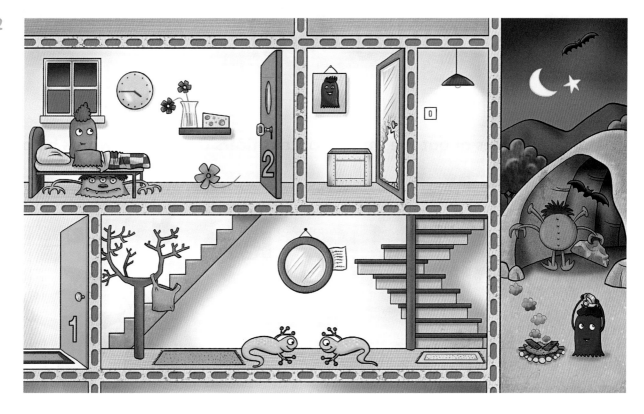

C **Say what has happened in picture 2. Complete the sentences.**

With the silver key, the player ....*has opened*.......... the second door.

1   The player .... the glass door.
2   Someone .... on the light.
3   The player .... the box that's made of wood on the fire.
4   The monster .... back into its cave.
5   The player .... the gold ring!

D **Find and write Ben's correct answers.**

Vicky: It's a good game, but I think it's for younger children.
Ben: 1 ....
Vicky: How long did it take you to get the gold ring?
Ben: 2 ....
Vicky: Which part of the game did you enjoy the most?
Ben: 3 ....
Vicky: Shall we play it one more time?
Ben: 4 ....

A   If you want, or we could play my game.   E   That happens in the middle of the game.
B   I don't know. I didn't look at my watch.   G   But you aren't old enough.
C   When the player broke the door!   H   No, that's the third one.
D   I took it all the way to the fire.   I   Well, I enjoyed it and I'm ten.

E **What must the second player do?**

37 Exciting days!

A Make sentences about the things police officers do. Use the words below.

centre
trousers
problems
car parks
missing
exciting
jacket
car
lost
city
police
uniform
blue
police officer
things
information
station
traffic
job
dangerous
visitors
helps

B Read the text and write the missing words. Write one word on each line.

Example | David is 44. He's ....*a*.......... police officer and works at the police
1 | station which is one of .... highest buildings in the city centre.
2 | Every morning, he gets up at six o'clock and .... on his uniform. He has to wear blue trousers, a special jacket and a blue hat.
3 | When he arrives at work, he asks for information .... anything that has happened during the night. After that, he gets into his police
4 | car. Every day .... different. He might stop traffic problems at the shopping centre, help people find car parks or show visitors the way
5 | to somewhere. He also tries to catch people .... drive too fast, of course. It's an exciting but dangerous job.

C Choose a job and complete the boxes.

Name: ....

What/job?	....
When/get up?	....
What/wear?	....
Where/work?	....
Age?	....

Name: ....

What/job?	....
When/get up?	....
What/wear?	....
Where/work?	....
Age?	....

D ▶ **An afternoon at the fire station. Listen to Jim.**
Write numbers 1–4 in the boxes next to the pictures.

This is me coming down from the fire station to the .... inside a large kind of slide that's made of .... I can't stop ....!

These are some of the .... from my class in the fire station. We're wearing the firefighters' helmets – my teacher has put one on too! And look! I'm .... in some boots and in a firefighter's .... ! I love it – but it's enormous. Look!

Now we're getting really .... because we're playing with the water from the ....!

This is Miss Night and our ....*class*............ . We're waiting outside the .... to the fire station. There's lots to see and .... , so we're all feeling really excited!

E **Complete the sentences under the pictures with words from the box.**

~~class~~ wet jacket ground entrance passenger students learn
wifi work traffic laughing dressing up plastic fire engine

38 Famous people

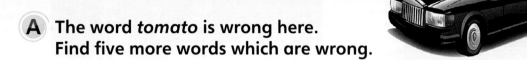

A The word *tomato* is wrong here.
Find five more words which are wrong.

1 Bill <u>tomato</u> writing adventure stories and dreams of being a famous journalist
2 like his mother. Last Tuesday, Bill was playing in the street with a group of
3 friends. Suddenly, a black understood with large, dark windows stopped and a
4 woman got out.

5 'I'm classroom that's the queen!' Bill whispered, but his friends didn't believe
6 him. Then the woman came over and said, 'Hello, we've got a problem with
7 the engine. Is there a good mechanic near here?' 'There's one just around the
8 yellow,' answered Bill. 'Could you take us there?' asked the woman.

9 Bill showed them the way. After he fixed the car, the mechanic said, 'Excuse me,
10 aren't you the queen?' The woman trousers, 'Yes! Thank you very much for
11 helping us.' The mechanic took a photo of Bill with the queen and a week later,
12 a downstairs from the queen arrived. Bill used that and the photo to write a
13 story for the town newspaper.

B Where do these words go in the story?

likes   letter   smiled   corner   car   sure

Choose the best name for the story. Tick (✔) one box.

An important person visits our town ☐

Bill asks a mechanic to repair his car ☐

A trip to the concert with the queen ☐

C Write 1, 2, 3 or 4 words to complete each sentence.

Example   Bill's mum is .

1   The windows of the car that stopped near Bill were large and
    ....
2   When Bill said. 'I'm sure that's the queen!', his friends ....
    him.
3   The queen wanted to know where she could find ....
4   The queen thanked the mechanic for .... them.
5   Someone took a picture of .... that day.
6   A week later, the postman brought Bill .... from the queen.
7   Bill wrote a story for .... about the day the queen visited
    the town.

D Read the queen's diary. Write one word on each line.

Example
1
Earlier today I went to .... *visit* .... a new museum that was about 100 kilometres away. My driver .... me there in the car.

2
On the way home, the car started making strange noises, so we decided .... find a mechanic quickly.

3
We saw a .... in the street with some friends and he

4
knew a mechanic .... worked just round the corner.

5
Tomorrow morning, I'll send him a letter to thank him .... helping us!

E ▶ Look at the pictures and listen. Tell the story.

Sue and Alex go to the match

1
Alex—
Sue—

2

3

FOOTBALL CLUB

4

5

F Write your answers to these questions.

1   Which famous person would you like to meet? ....

2   Why is this person famous? ....

3   Why do you like this person so much? ....

4   What does this person look like? ....

5   Would you like to be famous one day? ....

81

39 In villages and towns

A You're walking through a village. What can you see?

B Read the story. Choose a word from the box. Write the correct word next to numbers 1–5.

> Example
>
> full   dinner   huge   feed   tent   thanks   stamps   frightening   score   sold

Mrs Forest works in the village post office. No one knows if she's 75, 85 or 95, but she's very old. The post office is the most popular place in the village. It's always ....*full*........ of people, so Mrs Forest can ask lots of questions.

Daisy Cage came in to buy six (1) .... 'What was your camping holiday like, Daisy?' Mrs Forest asked. 'What an adventure! Did you like sleeping in a (2) .... ?'

Pat Down needed some brown paper. 'Hi, Pat!'' Mrs Forest said. 'You've (3) .... your motorbike, haven't you? What will you buy with all that money?'

It was Mrs Forest's birthday last Saturday. Her husband came into the post office and gave his wife a big red balloon. 'How lovely!' she said. Then Mr Forest took a (4) .... pizza out of his bag. Would you like this or something else for your birthday (5) .... ?' Mr Forest liked asking lots of questions too! 'Chocolate cake, David!' Mrs Forest answered with a big smile.

6 Now choose the best name for the story. Tick (✔) one box.

Mrs Forest makes a pizza! ☐   More and more questions! ☐

Pat's special birthday present! ☐

C ▶ What did Lucy's mum buy in each place? Listen and write a letter in each box.

chemist's   hospital   bus station   shopping centre   sports shop   clothes shop

A   B   C   D   E   F   G   H

D Find words in each wheel. What are the three places in town?

E What's this? Choose the correct words and write them on the lines.

a restaurant   a flashlight   a journey   an entrance

Example	You can sit here and eat a meal that a cook has made for you.	*a restaurant*
1	People make things like computers or phones or fridges in this kind of place.	....
2	This has two wheels and you can ride it from one place to another in the town or countryside.	....
3	Two people can sit on this to move quickly down a hill but there must be snow on the ground!	....
4	People go to this to hear music and watch people playing instruments on a stage.	....
5	This is all the cars, trucks, lorries and motorbikes we can see on a busy road.	....
6	If you remember to take this with you, you can turn it on and see better in dark places.	....
7	When you go from the street to the inside of a building, this is what you walk through.	....
8	People who enjoy doing this like sleeping in a tent more than in a hotel room.	....
9	Footballers in each team are always trying to score these during the match!	....
10	This means the same as travelling from one place to another.	....

goals   traffic   a seat

a sledge   offices   railway   a factory

a concert   camping   a bicycle   snowboarding

F *Funtime* Play the game! Guess the describing word.

40 What a strange planet!

> **A** Read the story. Write some words to complete the sentences about the story. You can use 1, 2, 3 or 4 words.

Wonderful sounds

Hello, my name's Tom and I live in a busy city, but last June I went camping in the countryside for the first time. I went with Grandpa Pat and my two cousins who are three years older than I am. It was exciting because we didn't arrive until midnight. It was very quiet and we couldn't see very much because it was so dark. Putting up our tent was quite difficult!

When I woke up early the next morning, there were so many unusual sounds outside. I could hear birds that were singing all kinds of different tunes. I could also hear some water outside, but it sounded much noisier than a river. I opened up the tent quietly because I didn't want to wake my grandfather and cousins and stood up slowly to see where we were. 'This is the most beautiful place that I've ever seen!' I thought. 'I can't wait to walk up those hills and through those woods.'

Then, between some high trees, I saw the lovely waterfall and all the rocks below it. There was a deep stream too. It was only a little way away from our tent. 'What a beautiful view and that's such a wonderful sound,' I whispered to myself. 'I wish I could see and hear this every morning!'

Examples

Tom went camping last June with his grandfather and his two .... *cousins* ....

Tom was three .... *years* .... younger than his cousins.

Questions

1   It was already dark when they put up the tent because they arrived at
    ....

2   Tom could hear lots of wonderful sounds when he woke up the
    ....

3   One of the sounds came from something that was louder ....

4   Tom didn't want to wake the others up so he quietly .... and went outside.

5   Tom thought the hills and woods looked more .... than any other place he knew.

6   Not far from their tent, Tom could see some rocks below a ....

7   The mountain stream was making .... that Tom wished he could hear it and see this view every morning.

B What's unusual about the animals in this picture?

C ▶ Listen and answer the questions about the competition.

Which place would you like to visit?

What's the most beautiful sound that you've ever heard?

What's the best photo of an animal or place that you've ever seen?

D Look at the three pictures. Write about this story. Write 20 or more words.

E *Funtime* Do the world quiz!

41 Meet the pirate actors

A Write the correct words on the green lines and the correct names on the pink lines.

shorts   air   costume   made   never   light   wheel   pushes   wished   dangerous

1   In the film, ...William.... is never lazy. He looks after the ship's flags and tidies the kitchen. He's wearing swimming .....shorts..... with red stars on them.

2   William's grandfather, whose name is .... spends lots of time fishing. He has dressed up in an old red and white striped T-shirt. One of his legs is .... of wood! He thinks he's the best actor in the film!

3   William's sister's name is .... She's got a noisy pet parrot and she .... wears shoes in the film! Can you see her toes?

4   .... is William's grandmother. She does the cooking on the ship and has to sing a lot in the film. Part of her .... is a pair of pink gloves.

5   William's father, ..., is busy all day. He counts his money, watches the sea for .... sharks and tells everyone what they must do! But he sometimes forgets what he has to say in the film!

6   William's mother never takes her spotted hat or silver necklace off. She sails the ship at night in the bright .... of the moon. Her name is ....

B ▶ **Listen and colour and write.**

C **Let's talk about swimming.**

When did you learn to swim?
Where can you go for a swim?
Who taught you to swim?
Tell me more about a beach or a swimming pool that you know.

D **What was each person doing when the photographer took these photos?**

hiding behind a pyramid   holding a sweet puppy   eating some special pasta
collecting lovely shells   climbing a rock   riding a friendly camel

E **Think hard! How much can you remember?**

42 Holiday news

A ▶ **What has Mary already done? Tick (✔) the boxes.**

B **Read the email that Mary is going to send to her family.**

Dear Mum and Dad,

I'm sorry that I haven't written to you earlier, but don't worry. I'm fine and we're having a great time. This is only a short email because I've got to hurry. We're going to visit the pyramids today! I hope you like this picture of us in the desert! I'll send you some more photos soon. Betty took a good one of me in the entrance to our hotel and another of us all in the pool.

See you on Saturday. Our plane will arrive at about three o'clock so I'll get my backpack and meet you at the passenger exit at about a quarter to four.

Lots of love, Mary

C ▶ **Look at Mary's photo. Listen and draw lines.**

Matt   Sarah   Hugo

Katy   Betty   Alex   Harry

D Look at Mary's other photo. What differences can you see?

E Read the postcard and write the missing words. Write one word on each line.

Dear Nick,

We've already been here ....for........ *four days! There*

Example

1 .... *so many amazing things to see here! We've already*

2 *visited a museum* .... *had gold toys and strange clothes in it. We've been to the theatre too. I understood the actors because*

3 *they* .... *in English. The story was about a famous queen*

4 .... *lived 4,000 years ago.*

5 *This evening, our teacher is going to take* .... *and my classmates to a restaurant that's outside the city and I'd*

6 .... *to wash and dry my hair and change my clothes! I have*

7 .... *go now. See you next week at school.*

Mary

F Make sentences about the things you've done today.

43 Have you ever ...?

A Write the words to complete the questions.

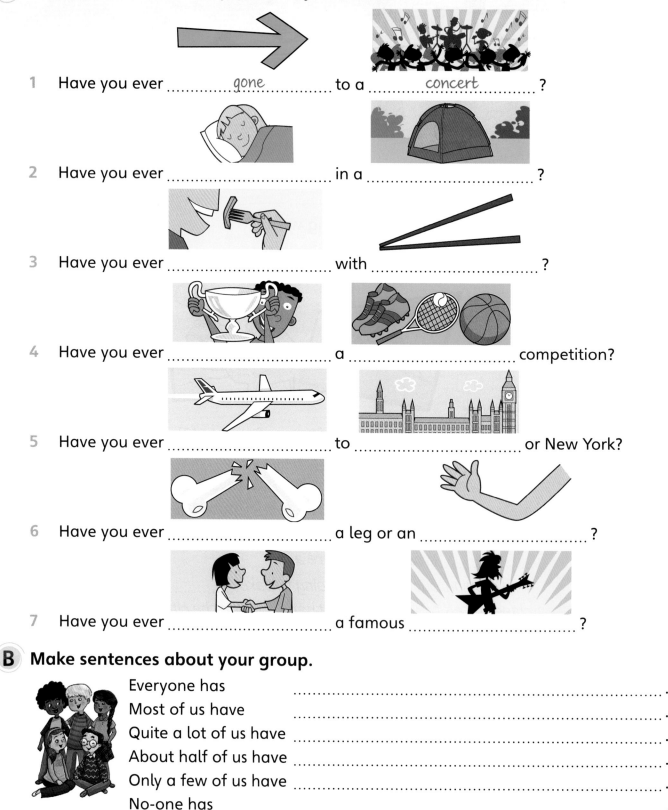

1 Have you ever ....gone............ to a ....concert............ ?

2 Have you ever .... in a .... ?

3 Have you ever .... with .... ?

4 Have you ever .... a .... competition?

5 Have you ever .... to .... or New York?

6 Have you ever .... a leg or an .... ?

7 Have you ever .... a famous .... ?

B Make sentences about your group.

Everyone has ....

Most of us have ....

Quite a lot of us have ....

About half of us have ....

Only a few of us have ....

No-one has ....

C Read about winter sports. Choose the right words and write them on the lines.

Winter sports

Example	Have you ....*ever*........ skied down a mountain? Skiing is an exciting sport but it isn't a new one.	yet before ever
1	.... are several old paintings on rock	1 We There They
2	walls inside caves that show people	2 what who whose
3	are skiing. Some of .... cave paintings are more than 5,000 years old!	3 these this that
4	About 180 years ago, on a small farm in the mountains, Sondre Norheim's father .... wood from the forest to make his young son a pair	4 use used using
5	.... skis. Sondre loved putting on his skis, jumping off the roofs in his village and skiing	5 by with of
6	down the hills. .... he grew up, Sondre made the first skis that could turn on soft snow and	6 How Why When
7	won .... important skiing competitions.	7 one many another
8	People still .... Sondre 'the Father of Skiing'.	8 call calls calling
9	Now, both skiing and snowboarding are really popular sports! Lucky families can stay in wonderful mountain villages where ski lifts take .... to the top of the mountain so they can ski	9 them him their
10	.... snowboard back down again!	10 if or because

D ▶ Look at the three pictures. Write about this story.

E Let's talk about things we've all done!

44 What has just happened?

A Read the two party invitations.

Hi!
Please come to my party on Saturday, 12 December at the Concert Café.
It starts at 5 pm.
Choose between pizza or burgers!
Make sure you bring trainers because we'll play football later!
Love, Emma

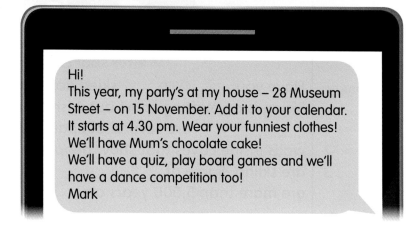

Hi!
This year, my party's at my house – 28 Museum Street – on 15 November. Add it to your calendar. It starts at 4.30 pm. Wear your funniest clothes!
We'll have Mum's chocolate cake!
We'll have a quiz, play board games and we'll have a dance competition too!
Mark

Write about the parties in these boxes.

Emma's birthday party

Date?	12 December
Time/start?	
Place?	
What/eat?	
What/wear?	

Mark's birthday party

Date?	15 November
Time/start?	
Place?	
What/eat?	
What/wear?	

B Read the conversation and choose the best answer (A–H).

Example   Jill: It's your birthday today, isn't it, Mark?

     Mark: ....F....... .

1   Jill: Are you going to have a party?

     Mark: ....

2   Jill: Have you invited all the kids in your class?

     Mark: ....

3   Jill: And what time does it start?

     Mark: ....

4   Jill: Has your mum bought a lot of food?

     Mark: ....

5   Jill: Have a good time!

     Mark: ....

     Jill: Next time, please invite me too!

A	At five, I think. I'm not sure.
B	Yes, we've just got some.
C	Yes, she's here today.
D	Happy birthday!
E	Thank you. I will!
F	That's right. I'm twelve. Example How did you know?
G	Yes. I'm really excited.
H	Only about ten of them.

C **Look at the picture in D.**
Try to find something for each letter of the alphabet.

Examples   a ......*armchair*......   b ......*bookcase*......

D ▶ **Listen and draw lines.**

Clare   Tom   Helen   Fred

Robert   Alice   Mark

E **Read Mark's diary and write the missing words.**
Write one word on each line.

TUESDAY 15 NOVEMBER

Example   I was twelve ......*years*...... old today. I got some excellent

1   presents! Ten .... my friends came to my party.
Tom gave me a computer game called 'Bats in your basement!'

2   I haven't tried to .... it yet, but it looks good. Sally

3   bought me a T–shirt. .... 's got an alien on the front! I
got a new keyboard from Mum and Dad. But Uncle Frank gave

4   me .... most amazing present. He's just given me a
sweet little puppy with long, soft, gold-coloured fur! I'm going

5   to .... it 'Honey', I think! It's playing with a toy penguin
at the moment! It's brilliant.

F *Funtime* **Play the game! Find your partner.**

93

45 Talking about the time

A Look at the boxes, read the sentences and write or colour.

.... ☐	.... ☐	March ☐	.... ☐
May ☐	June ☐	.... ☐	.... ☐
September ☐	October ☐	November ☐	.... ☐

1 Write the names of the six missing months on the lines.
2 How long is each month? Write the number of days in the small boxes.
3 Write today's date in the correct month box.
4 Write your birthday in the correct month box.
5 Colour the summer months bright yellow and the spring months bright green.
6 Choose colours for the autumn and winter months. Another way of saying 'in the autumn' is 'in the ....'.
7 Draw a star in your favourite month on the calendar.

B ▶ Listen and tick (✔) the box.

Which place did Richard and his class visit this year?

A ☐   B ☐   C ✔

1 When did Richard's school holiday begin?

APRIL 29   JUNE 4   SEPTEMBER 18

A ☐   B ☐   C ☐

2 What did Richard do on holiday?

A ☐   B ☐   C ☐

3 What did Richard bring home?

A ☐   B ☐   C ☐

4 When can Richard's aunt watch the holiday film?

A ☐   B ☐   C ☐

5 What will Richard wear?

A ☐   B ☐   C ☐

C Read the text. Choose the right words and write them on the lines.

Time

The Earth takes 365 and a quarter days to ....Example....move....... around the sun, so every four years we have a 'leap' year. In a leap year, 1 .... are 366 days so we 2 add another day .... February. You will see this on calendars and in diaries.

3 Most months have 31 days, but four .... the months only have 30 days. February is the 4 month .... only has 28 or 29 days. 5 Twice a year, ... countries in the world decide to change the time by one hour. We do this 6 .... we want to use more light from the 7 sun. This helps people who .... outside. This is also better for people that have to do 8 .... lot of driving.

We change the time twice a year. In March, we make the time one hour later and in October, one hour earlier. So, on the first day after the clocks 9 .... changed in October, 10 .... can stay in bed for another hour!

Example	moving	moved	move
1	there	those	they
2	to	with	over
3	from	of	with
4	whose	which	what
5	many	much	lots
6	because	than	but
7	working	works	work
8	the	a	any
9	have	has	having
10	he	we	it

D Do the train timetable quiz!

Jacktown	08:30	09:15	11:10	12:30
Fallwing	09:05	10:15	11:45	13:30
Letmore	09:55	10:55	12:35	14:20
Keepfield	10:10	11:25	12:45	14:45
Endwich	11:15	12:25	13:40	14:55

1 How many stations will my train stop at after I get on it at Jacktown and before I arrive at Keepfield? ....

2 How long is the journey to Keepfield if I leave Fallwing on the eleven forty-five train? ....

3 It's five past two. How long must I wait on the platform at Letmore station until the next train arrives? ....

4 I must arrive in Endwich by twenty past eleven. Which train must I catch from Letmore station? ....

5 I want to travel from Jacktown to Endwich on the fastest train. What time does it leave? ....

6 If I leave Jacktown station at a quarter past nine, spend an hour in Keepfield, then catch the next train to Endwich, what time will I arrive? ....

46 We're all at home today

A ▶ Who's talking? Match the numbers and letters.

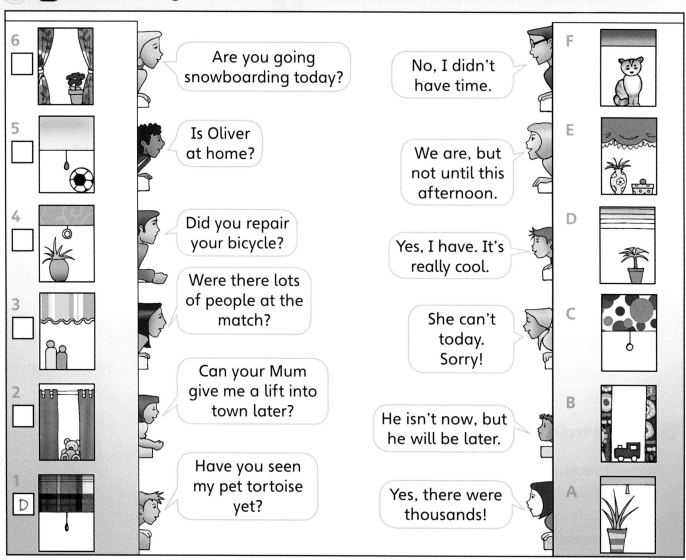

6 ☐
5 ☐
4 ☐
3 ☐
2 ☐
1 D

Are you going snowboarding today?

Is Oliver at home?

Did you repair your bicycle?

Were there lots of people at the match?

Can your Mum give me a lift into town later?

Have you seen my pet tortoise yet?

No, I didn't have time.

We are, but not until this afternoon.

Yes, I have. It's really cool.

She can't today. Sorry!

He isn't now, but he will be later.

Yes, there were thousands!

F
E
D
C
B
A

B ▶ Where has Sophia's mum put Sophia's things? Listen and write a letter in each box.

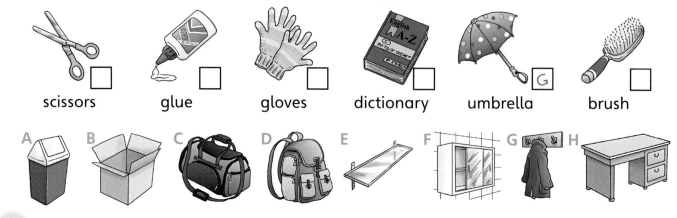

scissors ☐   glue ☐   gloves ☐   dictionary ☐   umbrella G   brush ☐

A   B   C   D   E   F   G   H

C **Read the story. Write some words to complete the sentences about the story. You can use 1, 2, 3 or 4 words.**

Naughty Daisy

Last Sunday, our family wanted to go to the village festival, but the weather was very cold and windy so it wasn't a good day to be outside. We decided to stay at home.

After lunch, my little sister Daisy was really bored. She came into my bedroom and said, 'George, play this board game with me!' 'Sorry, Daisy,' I said, 'I can't close these files on my laptop yet because I need to finish my science homework.'

Daisy went into the living room. 'Will you play with me, Dad?' she asked. 'Yes, but I'm busy now,' he explained. 'In a minute, but I must finish reading this important information on your school's website first.'

Mum was talking on the phone in the hall. Daisy began asking her to come and play, but Mum said, 'Not now, Daisy. I'm explaining something to Aunt Sarah.'

'No-one wants to play with me,' thought Daisy. She was really angry. She didn't like playing all alone so she went upstairs to fetch her favourite doll.

When Dad finished his work, he called Daisy's name. Then Mum finished speaking to Aunt Sarah and called Daisy's name, too. But Daisy didn't answer. I stopped writing and ran downstairs really quickly. I could hear her laughing loudly. 'She's in the kitchen by herself,' I thought. 'What's she doing in there … ?'

Examples

The family didn't go out because it was ...very cold and windy... outside.

That afternoon, Daisy was feeling very ....bored.......... .

1 .... was was finishing some school work on a laptop.

2 Daisy's father was reading some .... on the internet.

3 Daisy's mum couldn't play because she was speaking to ....

4 Because she didn't want to be alone, Daisy went upstairs to find
   ....

5 When Daisy's mum stopped talking on the phone and .... ,
   she didn't answer.

6 George stopped what he was doing and .... when he heard
   Daisy laughing.

7 George didn't know what Daisy was doing in the .... !

D *Funtime* **Play the game!**

Can I come too / to / two?

47 I will or perhaps I won't

A ▶ **Listen. What might Sam be one day?**

1 Sam won't be a _____dentist_____ because he thinks that's a _____boring_____ job.
2 Sam might be an ambulance _____ but that's a _____ job.
3 Sam may be a _____ because he thinks that's an _____ job.
4 Sam says he will be a _____ . That's a really _____ job!

B **What are these children thinking? What about you?**

I _____ be a
_____ .

I _____ be a
_____ .

I _____ be a
_____ .

I _____ be a
_____ .

C **Choose your answers. Tick (✔) the boxes.**

In ten years …

1 I'll be
☐ at school.
☐ at university.
☐ at work.

3 I won't have
☐ any homework.
☐ any friends.
☐ any money.
☐ any problems.

5 I may have
☐ a huge castle.
☐ a motorbike.
☐ a spaceship.
☐ a racing car.
☐ a big island.
☐ a gold violin.

2 I'll live
☐ in another city.
☐ in another country.
☐ on another planet.

4 I'll be
☐ single.
☐ married.

6 I might be
☐ a businessman/businesswoman
☐ a designer.   ☐ a doctor.
☐ an engineer.   ☐ a farmer
☐ a film star.   ☐ a nurse.
☐ a firefighter.
☐ a pop star.
☐ a sports player!

D ▶ **What will Mrs Kind give to each of her friends? Listen and write a letter (A–H) in each box.**

Grace B

George ☐

Alex ☐

Michael ☐

Sarah ☐

Robert ☐

A

B

C

D

E

F

G

H

E **Answer me!**

Yes, I will.

I might.

No, I won't.

I may!

Will you travel to other parts of the world in space rockets in the future?

....

Do you think you will you travel to the moon one day?

....

Do you think you will have a conversation with an alien one day?

....

Do you think you will have to live on other planets in the future?

....

F **What will happen?**

99

48 Doing different things

A Write each word next to *man, woman, man or woman*.

wife
king
manager
grown-up
husband
queen
kid

man   ....

woman   ....

man or woman   ....

B Read about this actor. Choose a word from the box.
Write the correct word next to numbers 1–5.

Example

called   time   interested   tasting   future   important   touch   waterfall   movies   swim

Hi! Many of you may think I'm ......*called*...... Sue
Pepper but that's just the name I use for work. My
name's Zoe Short, actually! I'm 21 and an actor.
I've already been in several (1) .... but now
I'm working with my best friend, Jolly, on a new TV
programme instead. You can see it soon on Channel 12.

I often have to do quite frightening things while I'm
on unusual adventures. I might have to (2) ....
with scary sharks or jump across rocks below a
(3) .... for example. My adventures are usually
quite safe but some of them look really dangerous!

We were filming the programme in a place that's a
long way away last week so someone had to fly me
there in a helicopter every morning which was fun.
I felt really (4) ....!

When we aren't filming, I like spending some quieter
(5) .... at home on our farm. My husband and
I love horse-riding in the hills there.

6   Choose the best name for the story. Tick (✔) one box.

   Zoe, the actor ☐   Jolly's new helicopter ☐   Sue's wild horse ☐

C Read the note and complete Zoe's speech bubbles. Write 1, 2, 3 or 4 words.

We can't film the walk on Monday next week, Zoe, so you'll do the hot air balloon ride that day. You'll have an unusual train journey on Friday – more information about that later. The walk with wild animals (the one you wanted to do on Monday) will be on Thursday now. Sorry! And on Tuesday, you won't go sledging in the mountains. You'll have a rock climbing lesson. We've made sure you'll enjoy Wednesday. You'll spend that snowboarding.

George

On Wednesday, I'm going to go ....

And I'm doing the .... on Thursday now.

Monday will be exciting. I'm going up in a .... !

It's the .... on Tuesday.

But I'm going to go on .... on Friday.

D ▶ Listen and write.

Nick Silkwood visits our town

Example	Nick's son's name:	*Michael*
1	Son's address:	23 .... Street
	Nick	
2	Number of grandsons:	....
3	Age he started singing:	....
4	Instrument he plays best:	....
5	Song he likes most:	My ....

E Ask and answer questions about Jack and Lily.

F Tell me about another person!

49 Busy families

A ▶ **Listen and draw lines.**

Vicky   Sally   David   Lucy

Nick   Jane   Jack

B **Find the second half of each sentence and write it on the line.**

1   The girl with the long brush is helping .... *to tidy the room* ....
2   The woman is cutting some bread to ....
3   The girl with the pen is trying ....
4   Two girls in warm clothes are ....
5   The girl with the glue is trying to ....

> to do her homework   making a mistake   make more sandwiches
> repair the rocket   doing some shopping   making a snowman   ~~to tidy the room~~

C **Look at the three pictures. Write about this story. Write 20 words or more.**

D Finish the answers with too or enough and words in the snake.

1 'Why don't you go outside, Vicky, and brush away the snow for me now?'
'Because it's too cold outside and my coat .... , Mum.'

2 'Why didn't you finish reading your other school book, Lucy?'
'Because the story and pictures are .... , Mum.'

3 'Why don't you dress your dolls up in some different clothes, Jane?'
'Because their hats are too old, Mum, and their dresses ....'

4 'Why can't you make that rocket a bit taller, Anna?'
'Because this newspaper's too thin, Mum, and this glue ....'

5 'Why aren't you doing your art homework now as well, David?'
'Because, Mum, it's .... and this table isn't big enough.'

boringgoodnicebiginterestingdirtythickfunnydifficultprettyquietsmallnewstrongdryoldeasynoisy

E ▶ Listen! Write the missing words.

Mum: Wake up, wake up!
It's time to (1) ......go...... to school!

Fred: But I'm too tired. (2) .... back hurts. I want to
stay in (3) ....

Mum: No, Fred, no! You must (4) .... up now, it's late!

Fred: It's not. It's too early. I'm not going (5) .... !
I'm not going anywhere! There's a storm outside.
Listen! It's raining (6) .... hard and it's too
(7) ....

Mum: No, Fred, no! It's sunny (8) .... warm. It's a lovely
day and you're (9) .... holiday. You were having a
(10) .... dream!

F Look at these pictures. What differences can you see?

G Funtime Play the game! Guess my four things.

50 On TV

A ▶ Listen and write.

Example   Name: Richard ......Hudson......

1   Job: ....

2   Makes things with: wood and ....

3   Starts work at: ....

4   Works in his: ....

5   What making now: ....

B Ask and answer questions about Tony, Vicky, Alex and Kim.

C Peter Sun is talking to Grace. What does Grace say? Write a letter (A–H) for each answer.

Peter   Hello Grace! How are you?

Grace   ......C......

Peter   Have you just arrived in London?

Grace   ....

Peter   Why are you here?

Grace   ....

Peter   What's your new film about?

Grace   ....

Peter   How long will you be in this country?

Grace   ....

Peter   When will you finish filming your next movie?

Grace   ....

A   That's right. I got here at midday.

B   The life of a famous painter.

C   Hi Peter. I'm fine thanks. Hello everyone! Example

D   That's OK. I'm very interested in making films.

E   To make a new film with my husband.

F   Only a week. Our next film is about a jungle story.

G   Next spring, I hope.

H   It's really good, thank you.

D Read the text and choose words from the box for 1–5.

~~millions~~ should Channel turn film screen improve singers gate

Every Thursday, ...*millions*........... of people in villages, towns and cities (1) ....
on their televisions at 7:30 to watch Peter Sun's wonderful programme which is on
(2) .... Four.
If you enjoy learning about people who have some of the most exciting jobs in the
world, you (3) .... watch it too!
Each week, Peter finds out all kinds of different information about famous
(4) .... , band members, artists and exciting businessmen and women.
Tonight, Peter Sun's conversation will be with the (5) .... star, Grace Keys!
Don't miss it!

E Read Sam's email to Peter Sun and answer questions.

Hi Peter,
I went to the World Zoo today. Someone told me about
the new dolphin trainer who works there. Her name's
Alex Sugar. She's not famous like other people on your
programme, but she's very interesting and funny and so are the dolphins at the
zoo! But there's a problem. Alex Sugar can come to the film studio, but the dolphins
can't. So we'll have to take all our cameras and lights to the zoo and film her, the
dolphins and the programme there. Do you agree with that? Sam

F Look at the pictures and tell the story.

Peter and the dolphins

1
Peter
Alex

2

5

3

4

51 Here's my news

A Write the parts of Low Island School you can see.

a  b  c  d  e  f

the office ....

....

> the sports hall   the library   the computer room   ~~the office~~
> the playground   the dining room   the entrance

B ▶ Which parts of the school is Nick in? Listen and write letters from A.

Example d   1 ....   2 ....   3 ....   4 ....

C Ask and answer about Eva and Robert's hotel website information.

Eva Cook's hotel

Hotel noisy/quiet?	noisy
How many rooms?	27
Sport?	tennis
Internet/bedroom?	yes
What/see from/balcony?	coconut trees

Robert Brown's hotel

Hotel noisy/quiet?	quiet
How many rooms?	610
Sport?	swimming
Internet/bedroom?	no
What/see from/balcony?	car factory

D Read the two emails and the sentences in the large box. Who wrote each sentence? Anna or Fred?

Which sentences are from Anna's email? She's studying English.

Which sentences are from Fred's email? He's at the beach.

Text 1

@

Dear Ben,
Here is a picture of the school where I'm studying English.
Anna

Text 2

@

Dear Ben,
Here is a photo of the beach which is near our hotel.
Fred

1 a We've been here since Monday and I can see an island from my hotel room.
  b Everyone here is really cool, but I wish I was better at speaking English!

2 a I'm making friends which is good because sometimes we have to do projects together.
  b I met some other children in the pool and we stayed together all afternoon.

3 a Later today, we're going to play football in the park behind our classroom.
  b We usually have lunch in a café that's only ten metres from the sea.

4 a The grown-ups aren't as busy as us. They just sit in the sun for most of the day. Boring!
  b Some of the others prefer to stay inside in the computer room, but I don't.

5 a At the end of the day, the school lets us choose between sport and watching movies. My listening has really improved because of all the films I've seen here!
  b In the evening, we walk down the path to the sea and sing songs round a fire. I never feel alone here!

E ▶ Listen to Paul. He's talking about his day.

F Write about <u>your</u> school or news.

52 What a lot of questions!

A Complete each question with words from the box.

Questions	Me	
1 ....Who.... 's your luckiest friend?	....	....
2 .... do you go online?	....	....
3 .... have you been in this class?	....	....
4 .... times have you been on a theatre stage?	....	....
5 .... instrument do you prefer – the drums, the guitar or the violin?	....	....
6 .... scored a goal in an important match?	....	....
7 .... of holiday do you like best?	....	....
8 .... birthday in your family is it next?	....	....
9 .... tall are you now?	....	....

B ▶ Listen. Which questions from A does Holly's mum answer?

C Write your own answers, then ask a friend.

D Read the story. Write some words to complete the sentences about the story. You can use 1, 2, 3 or 4 words.

Harry and the difficult questions

Harry Doors loved learning. He had hundreds of books in his room at home and often searched the internet, as well to find out about jungles, the oceans, snails, pop music or anything else that he was interested in.

One day Harry's teacher said, 'Would you like to be on a TV programme, Harry? It's a competition on Channel 7 for the cleverest children in the country. You'll have to answer several difficult questions!' 'Yes! Of course!' Harry answered.

The next day, a man called Mr Silver came to the school with some important information for Harry about the competition. 'But before we do the quiz on TV, I have four questions. Are you ready, Harry?' 'Yes!' Harry whispered because suddenly the quiz sounded quite frightening! 'Good! Where's the River Thames?' 'In London,' Harry said. 'And what are a group of jellyfish or bees called?' 'A swarm.' Harry answered.

'Well done! What's 27 times 5?' '135!' Harry answered quickly.

'Great! Which is the highest mountain in the world?' 'Mount Everest and it's 8,848 metres high!' Harry was pleased. He knew all his answers were right.

'Excellent!' the man said. 'You're clever enough for the competition. Next Tuesday a taxi will bring you and your parents to Television House at six o'clock! Now, I just need to know your age. When's your birthday, Harry?' Harry was so excited he couldn't speak. 'Sorry!' he said. 'I've forgotten!'

Examples

Harry's surname was ....Doors.......... .

There were *hundreds of books* in Harry's room.

Questions

1   Harry used his books and .... to find out lots of things.
2   The first person to tell Harry about the .... on Channel 7 was his teacher.
3   The .... in Harry's country will be on the TV programme.
4   The name of the man who came to see Harry was ....
5   The man gave Harry some .... about the competition.
6   Harry was happy because .... to the man's questions were right.
7   But Harry couldn't remember the date of his .... !

E ▶ Listen and colour.

Finding your way

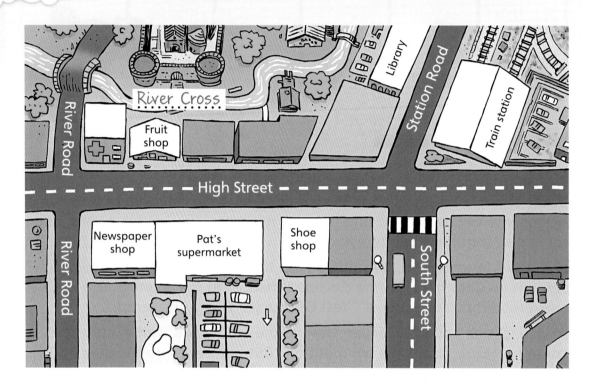

A Look at the map and read about Castletown. Find each place.

1. During your trip here, why not stay in Station Hotel? It's across the street from the railway station and next to the library in Station Road.
2. The bank is opposite the station and its car park. Its entrance is in South Street.
3. The post office is in High Street, across the street from Pat's supermarket.
4. There's a small sports shop on River Road behind the newspaper shop in High Street.
5. If you need to buy medicine toothpaste or shampoo, don't worry. There's a chemist on the corner of River Road and High Street. It's next to a fruit shop.
6. The bookshop is in the second building in South Street. It's got a very unusual green roof! The town centre bus stops are really near it.
7. Next to the post office, there's a restaurant called The Food Village. A path from its back door goes down to the river. People enjoy walking there.
8. You can use the wifi to go online in the Internet Café, on the corner of High Street and South Street.

B ▶ Listen and tick (✔) the box.

What does Harry need?

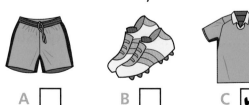

A ☐   B ☐   C ✔

1   What is opposite the library now?

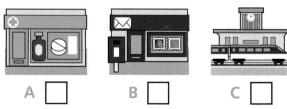

A ☐   B ☐   C ☐

2 Which way will Harry and his mother go to the castle?

A ☐   B ☐   C ☐

3 Which train will Harry and his mother take home?

A ☐   B ☐   C ☐

4 What will Harry have to eat?

A ☐   B ☐   C ☐

5 What has Harry lost?

A ☐   B ☐   C ☐

C Choose the correct words and write them on the lines.

a calendar   a festival   the internet   cartoons

a city

Example	There are twelve of these in every year.	......months......
1	This is information we watch or read. It is about what is happening in the world.	....
2	Our homes, large shops, schools, skyscrapers and factories are all kinds of these.	....
3	At this time of year it gets colder and leaves begin to fall from trees.	....
4	It is a good idea to walk or cycle along this when you are in a forest.	....
5	There are sixty of these every hour.	....
6	It is safe to cross a railway if you walk over this.	....
7	These are funny drawings that you can find in comic books.	....
8	You need to change this if you want to watch a different TV programme.	....
9	Some people put this on a wall so they can quickly see which dates to remember.	....
10	This is much larger than a town. Millions of people might live and work here.	....

autumn

months

the news

a path

minutes

a bridge   a channel   websites   midnight   buildings

D Ask and answer questions.

E *Funtime* Be actors in a shop or town!

54 Let's have some fun!

A Follow the lines to make suggestions.

Would you like   going to the funfair this evening?

Why don't we   playing my 'Frightening Creatures' game

Let's   invent a time travelling machine.

What about   to join that new rock music club?

Shall we   ask Dad to give us a lift into town?

How about   dress up in some funny old costumes?

We could   go snowboarding or skateboarding.

B Read the conversation and choose the best answer. Write a letter (A–H) for each answer.

Example

Paul: Hello! Is that you, Dan?

Dan: ......B......

Questions

1   Paul: I'm feeling a bit bored.

    Dan: ....

2   Paul: We could go to the Internet Café.

    Dan: ....

3   Paul: How about seeing the new 'Bad Mix' film?

    Dan: ....

4   Paul: What was it like?

    Dan: ....

5   Paul: Well, I haven't got any other ideas. Have you?

    Dan: ....

    Paul: OK!

A   I've already seen that.

B   Yes, it's me! Example

C   So do we!

D   Yes! Come to the park!

E   But that's such a boring place!

F   Quite good but a bit too long.

G   No, it wasn't like that.

H   Are you? Well, let's go somewhere.

D Look at the costumes in C and answer the questions.

1   What's the pirate wearing?   ....

2   What's the girl who's flying wearing?   ....

3   What's the queen wearing?   ....

Now choose answers to these questions.

1   What's does the message that's inside the envelope say?

    ....

2   What's on the piece of paper that the queen is reading? ....

    ....

3   What's on the man's piece of paper?   ....

E Shall we write a story? Read this first!

Bill and Mary's mother had to be at the theatre on Friday. She does an
important job there. Bill and Mary didn't want to go with her but they
didn't want to be alone and bored at home. They thought about doing lots
of different things but, in the end, they decided to climb up into the roof.
Their parents kept lots of old things in big boxes there. When their mother
came home, she was so surprised! Can you guess why?

55 If I feel bored

A **Draw lines between the two halves of the sentences.**

1 When I need to talk about something
2 If I'm feeling thirsty and need a drink
3 When I'm feeling really excited
4 If I'm feeling hot, I open a window or
5 When I'm ill, my mum brings me a spoon and

a I laugh a lot and sometimes sing.
b I phone my best friend.
c I get some water.
d I take my medicine.
e I turn on the fan.

B **Finish these sentences about yourself.**

1 When I'm tired, ...*I close my eyes and try to sleep for a few minutes.*......
2 I laugh when ....
3 I cry if ....
4 Sometimes I feel afraid when ....
5 If I'm bored, I usually ....
6 .... make(s) me angry.
7 On days when I feel lazy, I usually ....

C ▶ **Listen and say which picture. Then listen and say how picture 3 is different.**

1

3

D Read the story. Choose a word from the box. Write the correct word next to numbers 1–5.

> Example
>
> early   worry   disappear   race   deeper   blanket   pushed   faster
> suddenly   fell   knee

Alice and her father often go to the park together .... *early* .... in the morning. They're both going to be in a long (1) .... this summer so they go to the park to practise. Sometimes they run as far as five kilometres. On some days, Alice decides to roller skate or skip part of the way. She loves skipping and can skip (2) .... than anyone else in her class.

Last Monday, while Alice and her dad were on the path that goes around the lake at the park, an enormous furry dog suddenly ran past them and Alice's dad (3) .... into the water! He got really wet and cold and had to hurry home, quickly dry himself, find a (4) .... to put round his shoulders and sit down on the sofa.

'We can't run tomorrow, Alice,' he said. Alice felt unhappy when he said that because she loved running with her dad. Alice's dad could see that Alice was feeling sad. 'Don't (5) .... ! It will only be for one day!' he laughed. 'We can go again on Wednesday morning instead!'

Alice felt much better after that!

6 Now choose the best name for the story. Tick (✔) one box.

Be careful Dad! ☐   The skipping prize! ☐   Alice's terrible cold! ☐

E Complete the sentences about getting ready.

Before Mr (1) .... and his daughter, Alice, went to the park, they needed to get ready. Alice's father put on a (2) .... and some (3) .... and then he fetched his trainers from the (4) .... and put those on, too. Alice combed her (5) .... and put on her clean (6) .... and some (6) .... as well.

2

4

F Tell the story.

G *Funtime* Play the game! Which word?

56 Fun and games

Robert   Lucy   Michael

Have a   holiday!

Katy   Betty   Helen   William

B **Look at the pictures and tell the story.**

Helen teaches herself to waterski

1

Helen

2

3

4

5

C Robert's favourite word game.

gold	autumn	necklace	swim	tractor
cap	penguin	ski	beetle	minutes
red	puppy	engineer	draw	tomorrow
along	surprised	fire engine	purple	kiwi
taxi	black	lazy	designer	film star
near	bracelet	noodles	below	ambulance
yoghurt	midnight	Tuesday	trainers	sick
artist	olive	afraid	silver	zebra
hide	over	waiter	ring	cereal
truck	sore	donkey	dance	opposite

D *Funtime* ▶ **Now listen and play Betty's favourite word game!**

117

15 What's for dinner?

Learner A
Ask and answer questions.

Grace's cake

Whose birthday?	....
What/in/cake?	....
What colour/cake?	....
Where / Grace making / cake?	....
Grace's cake large/small?	....

20 Calling and sending

Learner A
Ask and answer questions.

Eva's new phone		Robert's new phone	
When/get?	two weeks ago	When/get	?
Colour?	silver	Colour	?
Big/small screen?	big	Big/small screen	?
Who/often call?	best friend	Who/often call	?
Where/keep?	in pocket	Where/keep	?
How many messages send each day?	27	How many messages/ send each day	?
How many tunes listen to each day?	15	How many tunes/ listen to each day	?

118

21 The time of the year

Learner A
Ask your friend these questions and write their answers.

What time of the year do you usually go on holiday?

....

Do you use a clock or a phone to wake you up for school?

....

What's your favourite month of the year?   ....

Which month is usually the hottest where you live?   ....

Where do you usually go at the weekend?   ....

Which century would you most like to live in?   ....

How do you remember important dates? Do you put them on your phone or calendar?

....

24 Leaving and arriving

Learner A
Ask your friend these questions and write their answers.

How do you get to school each day?   ....

How long does it take you to get to your favourite place in town?   ....

What's the most boring way to travel?   ....

Would you like to go for a ride in a racing car one day?   ....

What's best? Travelling on a motorway or along small, quiet roads?

....

15 What's for dinner?

Learner B
Ask and answer questions.

Tom's cake

Whose birthday?	....
What/in/cake?	....
What colour/cake?	....
Where / Tom making / cake?	....
Tom's cake large/small?	....

20 Calling and sending

Learner B
Ask and answer questions.

Eva's new phone		Robert's new phone	
When/get	?	When/get?	last year
Colour	?	Colour?	gold
Big/small screen	?	Big/small screen?	small
Who/often call	?	Who/often call?	granddaughter
Where/keep	?	Where/keep?	in kitchen
How many messages/ send each day	?	How many messages/ send each day?	1
How many tunes/ listen to each day	?	How many tunes/ listen to each day?	50

21 The time of the year

Learner B
Ask your friend these questions and write their answers.

When's your birthday? ....

How often does it rain where you live? ....

What's your favourite time of the day? ....

Which do you prefer: winter or summer? Why?

....

What's your favourite day of the week? ....

Do you prefer to tell the time with a phone, a clock or a watch?.................................

What date is the biggest festival in your city or country? ....

What do people do at the festival? ....

Do you have special food that day? ....

24 Leaving and arriving

Learner B
Ask your friend these questions and write their answers.

How do you travel into town? ....

How long does it take you to get to home from school? ....

What's the most exciting way to travel? ....

Would you like to explore space in a spaceship one day? ....

What would you like to learn to drive? ....

25   What shall we do next?

Learner A
Ask and answer questions.

Clare's school trip	
Where/now	?
Who/with	?
How/travel there	?
What/learning about	?
What/going to do next	?

George's school trip	
Where/now?	History Museum
Who/with?	favourite teacher
How/travel there?	school bus
What/learning about?	kings and queens
What/going to do next?	watch video

32   Where?

Learner A
What are these places?

1   People go to this place to watch their favourite team and

....

2   ....

learn about things from the past. ....

3   ....

you might go there if you need to catch a train. ....

4   When you are older and finish school,

....

5   These usually have lots of bedrooms and bathrooms and

....

35 What's it made of?

William's secret thing	
When/find?	last winter
Where/hide?	on top shelf in his cupboard
little/large?	large
What/secret thing?	strange key
What/made of?	gold

Sam's secret thing	
When/find	?
Where/hide	?
little/large	?
What/secret thing	?
What/made of	?

53 Finding your way

Learner A
Ask and answer questions.

How do you travel to the shops?
Who usually carries the shopping?
Which shops don't you like?
Tell me about your favourite shop.

25 What shall we do next?

Ask and answer questions.

George's school trip	
Where/now	?
How/travel there	?
What/learning about	?
What/going to do next	?
Who/with	?

Clare's school trip	
Where/now?	Science Museum
How/travel there?	train
What/learning about?	moon and stars
What/going to do next?	send text message
Who/with?	best friend

32 Where?

Learner B
What are these places?

1 ....
  people stay in them when they are away from home.   ....

2 ....
  players try to score goals.   ....

3 You might go here to meet passengers who have arrived
  on a train or ....

4 Families and history teachers sometimes take children here to

  ....

5 ....
  you can go to this place to study.   ....

35 What's it made of?

Learner B
Ask and answer questions.

William's secret thing	
What/secret thing	?
Where/hide	?
What/made of	?
little/large	?
When/find	?

Sam's secret thing	
What/secret thing?	beautiful comb
Where/hide?	in a box under her bed
What/made of?	silver
little/large?	little
When/find?	last summer

53 Finding your way

Learner B
Ask and answer questions.

Who goes shopping with you?
When do you go shopping?
What things do you like buying?
Tell me about your favourite shop.

48   Doing different things

Learner A
Ask and answer questions.

Jack's first job	
How old?	20
Who/work with?	older brother
What job?	firefighter
How/go to work?	motorbike
Hobby?	snowboarding

Lily's first job	
How old?	?
Who/work with?	?
What job?	?
How/go to work?	?
Hobby?	?

49   Busy families

Learner A
Who makes / does your bed each day?
Who does / makes the food shopping in your family?
Do you enjoy making / doing models of different things?
Do you hate or love making / doing science projects?
Are you good at doing / making different kinds of milkshakes?
Which do you prefer, doing / making school work on a laptop or tablet?
Which sports can you and your friends make / do in the summer?

41   Meet the pirate actors

Learner B
What was each person doing when the photographer took these photos?

> hiding behind a pyramid   holding a sweet puppy
> eating some special pasta   collecting lovely shells
> climbing a rock   riding a friendly camel

48   Doing different things

Write one family word in each gap.

1   My .... is the person that my uncle is married to.
2   My .... are my aunt and uncle's children.
3   After your eighteenth birthday, some people think you aren't a teenager.
   You are a ....!
4   I can say my .... to mean 'my mother and father'.
5   I can say my .... to mean 'my grandmother and grandfather'.
6   My mum is my dad's ....
7   My dad is my mum's ....
8   I am a girl so I am my grandfather's ....
9   My brother is my grandmother's ....
10   I can say my .... to mean the other children in my class.

48   Doing different things

Learner B
Ask and answer questions.

Jack's first job	
Hobby	?
What/Jack's job	?
How/go to work	?
Who/work with	?
How old/Jack	?

Lily's first job	
Hobby?	snowboarding
What/Lily's job?	photographer
How/go to work?	train
Who/work with?	uncle
How old/Lily?	18

49   Busy families

Learner B

Who makes / does most of your meals at home?

What kind of job would you like to do / make one day?

How do you feel when you do / make a silly mistake?

Do you hate or love doing / making quizzes and puzzles?

Where do you usually do / make your homework?

Which would you prefer to do / make, draw or paint a picture?

Which is the most interesting subject that you do / make at school?

14 Are you hungry? Thirsty?

25–30

Well done! You eat very well and you look after your body. This is important because at your age you are growing.

15–24

Come on! Some of the things you do and eat are OK, but you could look after your body better.

15 or less

Oh dear! You need to eat better food and to move your body more! Fruit and vegetables are very good for you. Eat fewer snacks and less fast food. Remember to sit down when you eat meals during the day – and don't forget that breakfast is a very important meal!

33 At the hospital

Harry	hurt	his	hand	when	he	was	hurrying	along the path.
							hopping	with the horses.
							helping	a hockey ball.
Helen		her	head	while	she		hitting	home.
								to the hospital.

Unit wordlist

1

sports and leisure
app
backpack
game
screen
skateboard
skateboarding
video games

clothes
glasses
jeans
sunglasses
sweater

colours
black
blue
brown
colour
orange
purple
red
yellow

school
roof
school
seat

transport
bicycle
bike
lorry
truck

other nouns
alien

verbs
find
get to school
like
play a game
repeat
ride a bicycle
think
wave

adjectives
round
square

2

people
king
queen

clothes
belt
boot
clothes
coat
crown
dress
glove
handbag
hat
helmet
jacket
necklace
pocket
ring
rucksack
scarf
shorts
skirt
sock

suitcase
trainers
trousers
umbrella
uniform
watch

colours
gold
green
silver

body and face
back
elbow
finger
foot/feet
hair
hand
head
knee
leg
neck
nose

places
castle
garden
wall

sports and leisure
piano

other nouns
letter
piece of paper
secret

verbs
carry
get (wet)
put on
tell (someone a secret)
wear

adjectives
amazing
blond(e)
important
little
wonderful

conjunctions
before
or
when

3

clothes
cross
shoe
spot
square
stripe

colours
gray/grey
pink
white

people
boy
children
girl
man
person/people
woman

body and face
beard
shoulder

leisure
model
newspaper
phone
towel

transport
board
flag
passenger

verbs
clean
listen to (music)
wash

adjectives
curly
fair
happy
sad
spotted
straight
striped
unhappy

4

names
first name
surname

family and friends
best friend
classmate
friend

work
singer

animals
dog
parrot
pet
rabbit

home
table

sports and leisure
guitar lesson

places
bus stop
corner
house
park
road
street

verbs
be called
be good at
dance
get off/on a bus
invite someone
to a party
live
look like
spell

adjectives
funny
loud
naughty
same
sweet

conjunctions
also
too

expressions
Hi!
See you!
Who else?

5

animals
animal
bat
bee
beetle
bird
butterfly
camel
carnivore
chicken
creature
crocodile
dinosaur
dolphin
donkey
fish
goat
insect
jellyfish
kangaroo
lizard
mouse
octopus
penguin
polar bear
swan
tortoise
zebra

body and face
fur
tail
tooth/teeth
wing

sports and leisure
cartoon

film
story book

places
jungle
science museum

other nouns
group
pair of
part of
place
problem

adjectives
afraid of
big
dangerous
extinct
friendly
frightened
furry
heavy
large
long
small
wild
wrong

verbs
disappear
eat
feel
fly
get (colder)
grow
hop
jump
mean
move
swim

conjunctions
but

prepositions
about
of

6

animals
eagle
elephant
fish
fly
giraffe
hippo
horse
sea creatures
shark
whale
zoo

clothes
T-shirt

possessions
brush
keyboard
snowboard
thing
violin

verbs
brush
buy
choose
go camping
hate
love
use

7

body and face
ear
eye
mouth

the world around us
country
east
farm
farmer
field
hill
north
south
west

animals
cow
sheep
sheep dog

food and drink
biscuit
cookie

transport
engine
tractor

time
early
evening
later
morning
today

verbs
believe
bounce
build
call
catch a ball
chat
clap
climb
come back
cook
cry

decide
drive
follow
guess
hear
help
hold
kick
laugh
look for
lose
make someone
must
pull
push
remember
run a long way
say
see
shout
sing
smell
speak
stop
throw
whisper
whistle

adjectives
excited
favourite
tidy
tired

adverbs
again
early
loudly
suddenly

conjunctions
after

expressions
Well done!

8
school
app
art
artist
class
competition
computer
drawing
English
fact
geography
history
homework
language
lesson
maths
music
numbers
paint
painting
partner
pencil
project
quiz
science
sport
student
study trip
subject
teacher
text
university

places
library
pyramid
town square

names
Miss

adverbs
more than

verbs
add
bring
could
count
do a project
find out
learn
look at
meet
paint
play
instruments
practise
should
show
study
teach

adjectives
clean
famous
interesting

conjunctions
if

expressions
Me too!
See you
tomorrow!

9
school
bin
book
bookcase
chair
classroom
cupboard
desk
dictionary

eraser
file
glue
pen
rubber
ruler
scissors
shelf
spelling

**sports and
leisure**
band
concert
music festival

time
calendar
date
day

materials
card

verbs
break
complete
cut
draw a circle
glue
forget
keep
information
make sure
put
repair
tick
try
understand

adjectives
difficult
easy
special
thin

expressions
It's a good idea
to ...

10
clothes
bracelet
swimsuit

animals
cage
kitten
snake

school
college
letter
(alphabet)
meaning
poster
word

**sports and
leisure**
comic

verbs
change
cross
get hot
leave

11
**the world
around us**
beach
desert
forest
island
lake
leaf
mountain
sand
shell
sky
stream

tree
waterfall

places
city
town
village

sports and leisure
blanket
camera
camping beds
chess game
puzzle book
tent
torch

verbs
camp
fall off
grow
have a wonderful time
need
take for a walk
walk up
would like to

adjectives
deep
empty
low
tall

prepositions
at the bottom of
by (near)
in
next to
on
round
under

expressions
How are you?
Is everything OK?
No problem!
Of course!
What about?

12
space
astronaut
Earth
Jupiter
Mars
Mercury
moon
planet
rocket
Saturn
sky
space
spaceship
sun
Uranus
Venus

colours
dark
light

the world around us
air
environment
map
robot
travelling

sports and leisure
badminton
golf
net
racket

other nouns
difference

numbers
degrees
twentieth

verbs
look like
move round
take photos/pictures
travel

adjectives
open

prepositions
around
near

expressions
All right!

13
weather
cloud
fog
ice
rain
rainbow
snow
storm
temperature
wind

sports and leisure
kite
playground
slide
swing

numbers
zero

people
kid

verbs
enjoy
go out
rain
snow

adjectives
bad
cloudy
cold
dry
fine
foggy
horrible
hot
noisy
sunny
terrible
warm
wet
windy
worse

expressions
Come on!
How about …?
Let's
Shall we …?

14
food and drink
apple
banana
bean
bread
burger
butter
cake
carrot
cereal
cheese
chicken

chips
chocolate
coconut
coffee
drink
egg
flour
food
fries
fruit
grape
honey
jam
juice
kiwi
lemon
lime
mango
meat
meatball
milk
milkshake
noodles
olive
onion
orange
pancake
pasta
pea
pear
piece
pineapple
pizza
potato
rice
salad
sandwich
sauce
sausage
snack
strawberry
sugar

sweets
tea
tomato
vegetable
watermelon
yoghurt

meals
breakfast
dinner
lunch

adjectives
delicious
hungry
thin
thirsty

verbs
be made of/
with
cook
drink
go to bed
have a dance
competition

adverbs
carefully
late

expressions
All right.
No thanks!

15
animals
bear
panda
spider

food and drink
fish fingers
picnic
teatime

time
Friday
Monday
Saturday
Sunday
Thursday
Tuesday
Wednesday

verbs
cut
fly away
mix
prepare
skip

adjectives
short
strong

adverbs
by yourself

prepositions
before
during

16
food and drink
lemonade
pepper
salt
soup

the home
bottle
bowl
box
CD
chopsticks
cup
cushion
fork
glass
knife

oven
plate
rug
spoon

work
break
email
office
office manager
program
project
room

verbs
answer an
email
close your eyes
dream
fetch
fix
go on holiday
mix together
pick up
prefer
taste
turn off
turn on

adjectives
asleep
closed
fantastic
open

adverbs
more than
so much

expressions
That's such a
good idea!

17
work
actor
cook
dentist
designer
doctor
film star
inventor
job
journalist
manager
mechanic
photographer
pop star

places
bookshop
café
car park
funfair
restaurant
stage
supermarket
theatre

**sports and
leisure**
front page
message
news
tablet
teddy bear
television
channel
TV programme

verbs
act
find out
get better
give something
back
happen

have a meal
make a film
make meals
write a letter

adjectives
best
busy
delicious
exciting
fun
light
worst

18
work
businesswoman
engineer
factory
internet
meeting

places
city centre
London

time
a.m.
clock
evening
half past
night
p.m.
quarter past/to
watch

other nouns
conversation

verbs
begin
come home for
lunch
design
finish

get up
go online
have enough time
send messages
start
talk to each other
visit

adjectives
different
first
funny (strange)
last

expressions
Oh dear!
My watch is wrong.
What's the time?

19
question words
how
how many
how much
how often
how old
what
what time
when
where
which
who
whose
why

family
grandma
grandpa
sister

animals
tiger

the world around us
pond

time
every day
soon

other nouns
middle
noise
visit

verbs
ask questions
explore
find answers
make someone angry
point
shop
stop doing something
use apps

adjectives
clever
enormous
huge
scary

20
the home
address
address book
dining room
e-book

sports and leisure
instrument
message
mobile phone

text (message)
tune
website
wifi

work
explorer

other nouns
hole
surprise

verbs
appear
be sure
call (phone)
chat
connect to wifi
email
end a conversation
get a text
go online
join a group
keep
make a video
open a programme
pay for
pick up emails
read an e-book
save phone numbers
search the internet
sell
send a text
sounds like
speak
win a prize

adjectives
sure
worried

expressions
Hooray!

21
time
autumn
century
fall (autumn)
hour
midday
midnight
minute
month
spring
summer
today
tomorrow
tonight
week
weekday
weekend
winter
year
yesterday

months
January
February
March
April
May
June
July
August
September
October
November
December

sports and leisure
festival

animals
baby animals

other nouns
another way (to say)

verbs
catch fish
fall
finish school
go to sleep
make a fire
make a nest
make a snowman
sail
start school
throw

adjectives
awake
lucky

adverbs
at the moment
fast
on the left
on the right

22
numbers
centimetre
hundred
kilometre
metre
thousand

sports and leisure
cinema
golf ball
golfer
movie

135

**the world
around us**
world

other nouns
birthday
birthday party
present
ticket

verbs
become
climb to the top
film
fly from
get married
hit a ball
pass a test
take (time)

adjectives
far
high
tall

adverbs
actually
only

pronouns
anyone
someone

23
work
business
laptop
machine
photo

places
entrance
exit

**the world
around us**
wave

verbs
arrive
borrow
collect tickets
enter a
competition
fall over
give someone
a lift
have a meeting
hurry
invent
join someone
for lunch
meet
open a
computer
programme
post
save a
computer file
search for
information
work

adjectives
double

adverbs
in the past

24
transport
airport
boat
bus
driver
helicopter
hot air balloon
motorbike
motorway

pilot
plane
platform
racing car
station
taxi
traffic
train
tyre
wheel

other nouns
adventure
money

verbs
be in danger
catch a train
cross
cycle
drop
explore space
get to a place
go by bike
go for a ride
go somewhere
on foot
have problems
wait (for)

adjectives
boring
quick
slow

adverbs
everywhere

prepositions
along

25
possessions
flashlight
toothbrush

other nouns
monster

verbs
clean your
teeth
go away
go on a
camping
holiday
have a snack
wash your
hands

adjectives
alone
brave
dirty
quiet
surprised
ugly

adverbs
next

expressions
It doesn't
matter.

26
**the world
around us**
ground

time
during the day
most of the
morning

**sports and
leisure**
holiday
hotel
pool
tour
view

clothes
baseball cap

verbs
go away
sit in the sun
stay in a hotel
tell stories
think

adjectives
great

adverbs
quite far away
then

**prepositional
phrases**
in the back of
the car

expressions
You're so lucky!

27
people
pirate

**the world
around us**
cave
rock
sea water

verbs
collect shells
get dressed
get ready
get undressed
go for a walk
hide
spend a long
time

adjectives
lazy

adverbs
perhaps
then

prepositions
after
until

expressions
Bye for now!
Cool!
Go away!
It's me!
It's time to go home!
Oh no!
Really?
What a wonderful place!
Wow!

28
sports and leisure
chess club
chess piece
first prize
funfair ride
gym
magazine
rain forest
silver cup
story competition
the end of the game

verbs
explain
get lost
go on a journey
hope
lift
move

stand
take someone to a place in your car
water
win a competition

expressions
Good luck!
I can't believe it!
Move out of the way!
Not now!

29
sports and leisure
baseball
basketball
bat
dancing
fishing
goal
hockey
ice skating
partner
player
sailing
skis
sledge
snowboarding
swimming
table tennis
team
tennis
volleyball
winner

health
bandage
x-ray

verbs
bounce a ball
feed
fish
hit a ball
improve
practise
pull
push
race

adjectives
dangerous
popular
safe
special

prepositions
across
behind
with

30
sports and leisure
bike race
cyclist
racing bike
snowball
snow sports

verbs
go up in a lift
sail boats
skate
take a taxi
win a race

adjectives
wrong

conjunctions
because
instead
so

while

adverbs
by myself
not yet

prepositions
without

prepositional phrases
on the fifth floor

expressions
I can't wait!
What a terrible mistake!

31
places
skatepark
stadium

sports and leisure
ice skates
music festival
roller skates
sports car

the world around us
land
ocean

verbs
play the drums

adjectives
interested
silly

32
places
bank
building
elevator

flat
market
roof
shop
skyscraper
stairs
steps

sports and leisure
board game

the home
bathroom
bedroom
grass

food and drink
candy

other nouns
shape

verbs
change
plant

adjectives
careful
heavy
light

prepositions and adverbs
ago
inside
outside

33
body and face
arm
face
stomach

health
ambulance
chemist's

cold
cough
earache
headache
hospital
medicine
nurse
stomach-ache
toothache

the home
comb
shampoo
soap

sports and leisure
tennis racket

verbs
break a leg
go red
have/take a temperature
have (got)
hurt
lie down
make
something stop
taste nice
touch

adjectives
better
broken
fine
ill
normal
pleased
sick
sore
well

adverbs
as (sick) as
badly
here

expressions
If you want!
Poor boy!
What's the matter?

34
sports and leisure
diary
football
practice
pop music
rock music
soccer

time
afternoon
morning

clothes
pyjamas

the home
painting

verbs
collect
feed
make sure
make us laugh
mind
ring
score
sledge
stay in hospital

adjectives
bored
cool

kind
OK

adverbs
a little
at first
only
quite
really
so (friendly)
still
very

prepositions
like

prepositional phrases
in hospital

35
materials
glass
gold
metal
paper
plastic
silver
stone
wood
wool

the home
card (computer)
mouse
envelope
fan
key
lamp
mirror
rug
window

sports and leisure
drum
toy

verbs
burn
come from

adjectives
flat
hard
untidy

adverbs
often
sometimes
usually

prepositional phrases
for a long time
in the middle of

36
the home
light

school
the opposite

verbs
mean
must

adjectives
first
old
second
third
young

adverbs
downstairs
quickly
slowly
upstairs

prepositions
above
behind
between
down
in front of
into
past
through
up

question words
how long (does it take)

37
work
fire
fire engine
firefighter
fire station
police car
police officer
police station

places
shopping centre
slide
visitor

other nouns
age

verbs
ask for information
dress up
lose
slide down
telephone
test
work

pronouns
anything
everything

38

sports and leisure
football club
match

work
postman
ticket office

verbs
get into a car
get out of a car
make a noise
smile
thank someone

adverbs
earlier today
just round the corner
one day (in the future)

expressions
Excuse me!
Thank you!

39

places
bus station
chemist
clothes shop
sports shop
stamp
store
sweet shop

the home
cooker
fridge
toothpaste

names
Mr
Mrs

sports and leisure
balloon

work
waiter

verbs
sell
shop
sleep in a tent

adjectives
full of
lovely

adverbs
always

pronouns
something else

expressions
Brilliant!
How much was it?

40

animals
cat
duck
frog
horse
lion
monkey
snake

food and drink
lunch box

sports and leisure
song
sound

the world around us
river
wood (forest)

verbs
could
film
put up a tent
sing a tune
wake someone
wake up
wish

adjectives
beautiful
fat
strange

adverbs
ever
quietly

prepositions
below

determiners
both
such

prepositional phrases
at night
for the first time

41

sports and leisure
costume
play (theatre)
ship
treasure

family
sister

body and face
moustache
toe

animals
puppy

the world around us
the light of the moon
star

work
cameraman

verbs
look after
sail a ship

adverbs
never

prepositions
under

pronouns
everyone

42

places
swimming pool

food and drink
ice cream

school
sentence

sports and leisure
postcard

verbs
change my clothes
dry my hair
have a bath
have a cup of

coffee
have a shower
have a wash
spend money
understand
wash (my hair)

adverbs
already

expressions
Dear (Nick),
I have to go now.
I'm sorry
Lots of love

43

sports and leisure
cave painting
ski lift
skier
skiing
skis

family
son

places
New York

verbs
call (name)
grow up
turn

adjectives
new

adverbs
down
ever

determiners
a few of us
all of us

139

a lot of us
both of us
half of us
most of us
some of us

pronouns
everyone
no-one

expressions
What fun!

questions
Have you ever
…?

44
the home
armchair
basement
radio
sofa

food and drink
chocolate
sauce
pie

other nouns
alphabet
front
invitation

verbs
choose
(between)
have a party
miss (a bus)

adjectives
right (correct)
soft

adverbs
just

expressions
Hello
Help!
Nothing else
for me!
Please

45
time
five o'clock
leap year
quarter past
twice a year

transport
railway station
timetable
train station

verbs
change the
time
stay in bed
stop at a
station

adjectives
missing
correct

adverbs
later

determiners
another
46
school
board

the home
apartment
flat
hall
kitchen
living room

**sports and
leisure**
sports centre

toys
doll

verbs
go out

adverbs
a bit later

pronouns
herself

expressions
In a minute!

47
work
ambulance
driver
dentist

verbs
have a
conversation
may
might
will

adverbs
in the future

**prepositional
phrases**
at school
at university
at work
on another
planet
48
**sports and
leisure**
hobby
horse-riding

hot air balloon
movies
rock climbing

**family and
friends**
aunt
brother
children
cousin
dad
father
granddaughter
grandfather
grandmother
grandparent
grandson
husband
kid
mother
mum
teenager
uncle
wife

people
grown up

transport
railway journey

verbs
have to

adjectives
frightening
several
unusual

49
other nouns
dream

verbs
do a project
do a puzzle

do a quiz
do homework
do some
shopping
do sport
do work
make a mistake
make a model
make
sandwiches
make your bed
tidy

adjectives
unkind
weak

adverbs
anywhere
(big) enough

expressions
Why don't
you..?
50
places
circus
film studio
gate
numbers
million

work
band member
dolphin trainer
golf player
horse rider
painter
train driver

daily life
life

verbs
agree

51

the home
balcony
DVD

places
computer room
dining room
gym
sports hall

school
home page
website
information

sports and leisure
dog sledge
line
ski teacher
ski team

other nouns
coconut tree
library card

verbs
improve
let

prepositions
since

expressions
Be quiet!
Boring!

52

animals
snail

numbers
times (27 x 53)

nouns
bit (a bit frightened)

verbs
forget
know

adjectives
ready

questions
What kind of?

expressions
Excellent!

53

places
bridge
market
path
post office
town centre

clothes
shirt

the home
door

numbers
millions

verbs
go past
go shopping
go straight on
turn left
turn right

prepositions
opposite
over

questions
How far?
Which way?

54

verbs
be in a race
feel better
go skateboarding
go snowboarding
hurry home
make me angry

adjectives
poor
rich

adverbs
somewhere

55

work
clown

verbs
comb (hair)
have an idea
roller skate

adjectives
cheap

adverbs
as well
together

determiners
a few

pronouns
something

expressions
Be careful!
Don't worry!

56

work
waiter

sports and leisure
water skiing
word game

school
crayon

the home
mat

verbs
cross out

adverbs
once

Irregular verbs

Verb	Past simple	Past participle	Translation
be	was/were	been	....
begin	began	begun	....
break	broke	broken	....
bring	brought	brought	....
burn	burned/burnt	burned/burnt	....
buy	bought	bought	....
can	could	—	....
catch	caught	caught	....
choose	chose	chosen	....
come	came	come	....
cut	cut	cut	....
do	did	done	....
draw	drew	drawn	....
dream	dreamed/dreamt	dreamed/dreamt	....
drink	drank	drunk	....
drive	drove	driven	....
eat	ate	eaten	....
fall	fell	fallen	....
feel	felt	felt	....
find	found	found	....
fly	flew	flown	....
forget	forgot	forgotten	....
get	got	got	....
give	gave	given	....
go	went	gone	....
grow	grew	grown	....
have	had	had	....
hear	heard	heard	....
hide	hid	hidden	....
hit	hit	hit	....
hold	held	held	....
hurt	hurt	hurt	....
keep	kept	kept	....
know	knew	known	....

Verb	Past simple	Past participle	Translation
learn	learned/learnt	learned/learnt	....
leave	left	left	....
let	let	let	....
lie down	lay down	lain down	....
lose	lost	lost	....
make	made	made	....
mean	meant	meant	....
meet	met	met	....
put	put	put	....
read	read	read	....
ride	rode	ridden	....
run	ran	run	....
say	said	said	....
see	saw	seen	....
sell	sold	sold	....
send	sent	sent	....
sing	sang	sung	....
sit	sat	sat	....
sleep	slept	slept	....
smell	smelled/smelt	smelled/smelt	....
speak	spoke	spoken	....
spell	spelled/spelt	spelled/spelt	....
spend	spent	spent	....
stand	stood	stood	....
steal	stole	stolen	....
swim	swam	swum	....
swing	swung	swung	....
take	took	taken	....
take off	took off	taken off	....
teach	taught	taught	....
tell	told	told	....
think	thought	thought	....
throw	threw	thrown	....
understand	understood	understood	....
wake up	woke up	woken up	....
wear	wore	worn	....
win	won	won	....
write	wrote	written	....